You Choose

James D. Williams

ISBN 979-8-88644-742-2 (Paperback)
ISBN 979-8-88644-743-9 (Digital)

Covenant Books
11661 Hwy 707
Murrells Inlet, SC 29576
www.covenantbooks.com

CONTENTS

Chapter 1 You Have a Choice 1
   Annette's Choice 1

Chapter 2 Your Choice Matters..17
   Adam and Eve...18
   Jesus...23
   Sowing and Reaping 28
   Follow Me...33

Chapter 3 Old Testament Choices...39
   Noah...40
   The 12 Spies...42
   Moses..46
   Naaman...49
   David, Bathsheba, and Uriah 51

Chapter 4 New Testament Choices..57
   Peter Walks on Water 57
   Saul's Conversion 61
   Ananias Goes to Saul 66
   Choosing Barabbas over Jesus 68
   The Women with the Issue of Blood........................72

Chapter 5 You Get to Choose (Part 1)......................................76
   To Serve the Lord..76
   To Seek the Kingdom of God 80
   To Submit and to Resist...86

To Guard Your Heart 91
To Be a Disciple 94

Chapter 6 You Get to Choose (Part 2) 99
Your Identity..99
Your Friends..106
Your Plans...110
Your Words 116

Chapter 7 Oops, You Made a Bad Choice 122

Acknowledgments 139

CHAPTER 1

You Have a Choice

I have heard it said that you are the sum of your choices made in the past. Other than choosing to read this book, think about all the choices you have made today. Choices can vary in importance. They can seem meaningless, or they can be a life-or-death choice.

Here is an incident told by my wife, Annette, that shows how a choice can be the difference between life or death.

Annette's Choice

When my daughter Candace was almost two, she loved to put everything in her mouth. She would eat anything and everything. One morning, I was in the bathroom, and when I came out, I noticed Candace standing over a small trash can in my room with a guilty look on her face.

The day before, I had cleaned out a jewelry cabinet and had thrown away some earrings that did not have matches any longer. One of those earrings was a button style that was missing the metal piece. The earring was a little bigger than a nickel, and it was blue.

I looked in the trash can and surmised that Candace had eaten that earring.

Now a couple of weeks or so before, I was reading a woman's magazine and read a story about a baby that was outside and ate a piece of bark, and the mom took her baby to the doctor and was told everything was fine. The next evening while sleeping, the baby died. The Holy Spirit brought that back to my remembrance.

I took Candace to her pediatrician; the doctor examined her and said that she was fine and that she would pass the earring in a few days. That did not sit well with my spirit. I had no peace. I told the doctor I was going to take her to the ER, so at the ER, they took an x-ray and didn't see anything, and they said that she was fine, but I insisted that since there was no metal on the earring that it might not show up on the x-ray, so after sitting around for hours, they did a barium x-ray and found the earring lodged in Candace's esophagus.

My husband, Candace's dad, sold surgical equipment to ENT doctors, so we ended up having an ENT surgeon come in and take out the earring, which meant a small surgical procedure and all the prep that goes along with that. It was a very long day as Candace ended up spending the night in the hospital.

The doctor who did the surgery said that if I had not insisted something was wrong that Candace would've gone to sleep and choked to death because that earring was lodged and was too big to pass through her system. When she lay down to sleep, the earring would have cut off her breathing.

Annette's decision to listen to the Holy Spirit and follow after peace and not follow the instructions of the different doctors saved Candace's life. Most choices in life are not this critical. Most choices in life are simple, others are more complex, and fewer are critical. The simple choices are like playing checkers. All the checkers move the same way unless a checker becomes a king. For example, it is a simple choice to choose between vanilla or chocolate ice cream when you don't like chocolate. The more complex choices are similar to chess. In chess, the different pieces move on the board differently, making combining moves for the desired result more challenging. An example of making a complex choice in today's world is the Global Positioning System (GPS). GPS systems are all about choices. Our lives often seem like the directions of a GPS. The address or result is where we want to be in life, and our choices are on the streets. Just as when following a GPS, we can get off course and have to be redirected in life. When redirected, we must make additional choices to get back on course.

In life, the choices we make have varying levels of importance. However, even choices that don't appear that critical can lead to unwanted results when chosen incorrectly. For example, bad eating habits can lead to being overweight and other problems. Nobody has ever become overweight because they overeat at Thanksgiving dinner once a year. The overconsumption of food the other 364 days of the year is the problem.

A good portion of the Bible is about God's choices and man's choices in response to God's choices. God chose to make man in His image. Man can chose to accept himself as the three-part being (spirit, soul, and body) that God made him, or like most men, they can view themself as a two-part being (soul and body). God chose to give to you and me His only begotten Son. Our response should be to choose (decide) to make Jesus our Lord and Savior. However, everyone does not decide to make Jesus their Lord and Savior, and thus they are not adopted into the family of God. When reading the Bible, I have found that most of the choices made are about trusting God and believing who God says they are and what they have through Jesus. If you aren't trusting and believing God, you will find yourself trusting this world, where Satan is the ruler, and only believing what you can see, touch, smell, taste, and feel.

There are many captivating verses and accounts in the Bible. These verses and accounts encourage the reader to choose to trust and believe in God and His promises. One such verse is Deuteronomy 30:19.

> I call heaven and earth as witnesses today against you, *that* I have set before you life and death, blessing and cursing; therefore choose life, that both you and your descendants may live. (Deuteronomy 30:19)

I like this verse because it is similar to a true-or-false question on a test. We all, at some time, have taken a test. Some of us may have had an instructor that wanted everyone in the class to receive a good score. To ensure that the class received a good score, the instructor told everyone the answers to the test before taking the test. God in Deuteronomy 30:19 is that type of instructor. God tells us the correct answer: "choose life, that both you and your descendants may live." The sad commentary is that even though God has given us the correct answer, most people choose death. In our life, we answer this question every day. The answer (choice) we give to this question every day shapes our lives and those that come after us. Making having a choice an essential cornerstone in every person's life. The thing about choices is that we make them every day, all day long. Sometimes we know that we are making a choice, but often we choose without realizing we are making a choice.

Having a choice is like gravity on the earth. It is something from which you can't get away. Gravity affects everything we do on earth, even when you don't notice the gravitational effect. For example, I play golf with some buddies every week. We play a scramble with two-man teams. While playing, we were at a 158-yard par-three, and the two guys we were playing against were on the green, and my partner was in the sand trap. My first decision is to play for the middle of the green and not at the flag. I want to make sure I am on the green.

Next, I must select what club to hit. I look at the elevation of the green; is it uphill, downhill, or level. Then I determine the direction and strength of the wind. I might even consider the temperature. There are many things to consider when selecting (choosing) a club. I select a club, and I take my shot, hoping I make a good swing. But the one thing that affects my shot more than anything else is the constant of gravity. I don't think about the gravitational effect on the ball because it is a constant. The gravitational effect is always there and always the same. Choices are always there, just like gravity. Choices affect our lives, and most of the time, we don't think about the fact that we have a choice or are making a choice.

Here is an example that everyone can relate to, at least in the United States. The United States is a capitalistic country. Although many seem as though they don't like it, capitalism is the most efficient way to distribute goods and services to the people who want or need those goods and services, and we participate in the system every day. Every time you buy (choose) a product, you vote or, should I say, choose for that product to be for sale.

A Philly Pretzel store opened up a few miles from my home when living in eastern Pennsylvania. One day, I explained to the owner how I was voting for his store to stay open every time I bought from him. When you spend your money, you vote for that product or service to continue. There have been times when I would discover a cereal that I liked, and shortly after that discovery, that cereal would be off the shelves. I and others had voted with our purchases for that cereal to continue being available, but our votes weren't enough.

Where I now live, one of the grocery stores has freshly baked bread every day. One day my wife bought a bread we had not tried before, Everything Bread. It is so, so good. When I went to the store to buy some Everything Bread, I discovered that they only have the bread when there is a special order for Everything Bread. I have since placed a special order of Everything Bread and have purchased it when others have made a special order. Because people kept ordering the bread, there is now a small quantity every day. As others and I chose to purchase Everything Bread, we told the store to have Everything Bread available, and now no special order is required.

As you can see, our choices affect us. But our choices also affect other people and things in the world. Because what we choose is important, we should know what it means to choose. Choosing is the act of selecting between two or more things (choices). We choose between material items, actions, and thoughts.

That means that when we must decide between two or more things, there is a choice to make. When driving down a road and coming to an intersection, you have to decide which direction to take (chose). Deciding which direction to continue driving in is easy when you know where you are going. But if you are lost, the decision is more complicated. You must choose whether to go straight, turn left, turn right, or turn around. However, there is a choice to be made. Even just sitting still at the intersection is a choice.

Even when you're being influenced or compelled by others does not overturn a person's free will to choose. Just because someone uses extreme forms of influence to get you to choose something they want, you still have the free will not to choose what they want. You might not like the consequences of your other choices and give in to the force. When you think about it, all our choices are influenced by others and circumstances.

Our God-given ability to choose is where we get our free will. You could say we have free will because we can choose. Even choosing between life or death can be a freewill act. Jesus said in John 10:18 that He laid down His life and that no man takes His life. In John 15:13, Jesus tells us that we can't express our love for another person more than to lay down our life for them. Both John 10:18 and John 15:13 show us that laying down our life for others is a choice. Daily we make choices that affect our lives. Sometimes others want to influence our choices, and at other times, they desire to force our choices.

Say you are a CIA agent kidnapped by a foreign country, and they want top secret information from you. What amount of force is required from them to get you to divulge the information they want? Would the threat of torture such as waterboarding work? Or would they have to use more physical forms of torture? Maybe you would give up the information for a large sum of money. Even if they threaten to kill you, you have a choice. You could suffer the consequences of not divulging the information and be executed. Even when you think there is no choice, there is a choice.

In the movie *Midway*, there is a scene where two men in the same situation make opposite choices. What happened is that the Japanese captured two US Navy sailors. The Japanese were searching for the US naval fleet, and they were determined to get that information from the US sailors. Remember, I am writing about the fact that there is always a choice in every situation. The two sailors are standing on the deck of the Japanese ship in front of the Japanese commander. Each US sailor had a long rope tied to one ankle and the other end of the rope tied to a weight. The one sailor looks the commander in the eyes and asks for a cigarette. They give him a cigarette. Now the commander believed that this sailor wasn't going to provide them with the location of the ships. So the commander had the sailor thrown overboard. He went down into the ocean and came up smiling. Then the Japanese threw the weight he was connected to overboard, and the sailor disappeared into the ocean. This sailor chose the lives of his fellow US sailors over his own life. The other US sailor, fearing death, started to cry and was willing to give the Japanese the information in an attempt to save his own life. The first sailor knew the consequence of not providing the location of the US ships and chose the consequence of death. The second sailor saw the consequence and wanted to avoid the consequence. The second sailor chose his own life over the life of his fellow US sailors. However, I don't believe the Japanese spared the life of the second sailor. The Japanese applied great pressure on both sailors, and they made their choice. But their choices were completely different. You, most likely, like myself, would like to think that you would make the choice that the first sailor made. But you honestly won't know until you are in the situation what choice you will make.

Let's look at Adam and Eve, who, in the same situation, made the same choice in Genesis 3:1–6 when they were in the garden.

> v. 1 Now the serpent was more cunning
> than any beast of the field which the LORD God

had made. And he said to the woman, "Has God indeed said, 'You shall not eat of every tree of the garden'?"

v. 2 And the woman said to the serpent, "We may eat the fruit of the trees of the garden;

v. 3 but of the fruit of the tree which *is* in the midst of the garden, God has said, 'You shall not eat it, nor shall you touch it, lest you die.'"

v. 4 Then the serpent said to the woman, "You will not surely die.

v. 5 For God knows that in the day you eat of it your eyes will be opened, and you will be like God, knowing good and evil."

v. 6 So when the woman saw that the tree *was* good for food, that it *was* pleasant to the eyes, and a tree desirable to make *one* wise, she took of its fruit and ate. She also gave to her husband with her, and he ate. (Genesis 3:1–6)

From reading this passage of Scripture, you will see that the serpent, controlled by the devil, didn't force Eve or force Adam to eat the fruit of the tree of the knowledge of good and evil. What the devil did was deceive Eve into choosing against God. Eve chose her fleshly desires over God's commandment and ate the fruit of the tree of the knowledge of good and evil. After she ate, she gave the fruit to Adam, and he willingly ate the fruit of the tree of the knowledge of good and evil, as a sheep led to slaughter. Verses 1 through 5 are where the deception took place. Satan got Eve to question what God had said, and then she chose to believe that God was holding something from them. Then Eve looked again at the fruit and saw that the fruit was good for food, pleasant to the eye, and would make her wise, and she chose to eat the fruit. Verse 6 informs us of something interesting about Adam. It says that her husband (Adam) was with her. So Adam was observing the conversation between Satan and Eve. Adam was probably thinking, *That sounds a lot like what God said. I want to be like God. That fruit does look good for food, it is a pretty fruit, and I would like to be as wise as God. Wow, Eve ate the fruit, and she didn't die.*

Thus, when Eve gave Adam one of the fruits from the tree, he chose also to eat. Then as James 1:15 tells us, when desire is conceived, it gives birth to sin, and when sin is complete, it brings death. Adam and Eve didn't die physically that day, but they did die spiritually. The DNA of Adam and Eve is in all of us. And just as Adam's and Eve's DNAs have been passed down in us physically, the spiritual defect of sin has been passed down in our spirit. Like Eve, we can be deceived and choose to do the wrong thing. I often think that people are like Adam and not deceived by others but give in to lustful desires. We see others doing what we want to do without any immediate consequences, so we choose to do it also. Because the consequences are not immediate, we think it will be okay. The consequences may not be immediate, but the consequences will come. Galatians 6:7 tell us that "whatever a man sows, that he will also reap."

Look at Joseph when he ran from Potiphar's wife in Genesis 39. Potiphar's wife had been attempting to seduce Joseph. I am sure she was pretty and desirable, but he chose not to succumb to the temptation. He realized that if he gave in to the temptation, he would be sinning against his master, who totally trusted him, and most importantly, he would be sinning against God. His choice was not to sin, which led to him being put in prison, yet he never regretted his choice.

You might read the account of Joseph running from Potiphar's wife and think, *He had a choice, but I don't have a choice about everything in my life.* You say, "I don't have a choice over my race, color, height, shoe size, or eye color." There are some things in the natural that you can't change or you can only change a little. If you were born Chinese, you are Chinese. If you are short, you are going to be short. You can take medications to grow and grow some, but you will not be seven feet tall. If you have blue eyes and want brown eyes, you could wear a brown contact lens. However, your actual eye color will still be blue. If you have a huge nose, you could have rhinoplasty to change the size of your nose. You didn't choose your biological family, but you can choose your friends. The point is that you came into this world with a biological design and in a certain environment that you didn't choose. There is only a limited amount of change that you can make to your design. But don't choose to let your design limit what you can achieve. God knows your original design, and it is perfect for His plan for your life.

I have shown you how important our ability to choose is and discussed the definition of *choice*. Now I would like to discuss how man received the ability to choose. To do that, I must go to the very beginning of man. I must go to Genesis 1:26.

> Then God said, "Let Us make man in Our image, according to Our likeness; let them have dominion over the fish of the sea, over the birds of the air, and over the cattle, over all the earth and over every creeping thing that creeps on the earth. (Genesis 1:26)

The AMPC Bible says it this way:

> God said, Let Us [*Father, Son, and Holy Spirit*] make mankind in Our image, after Our likeness, and let them have complete authority over the fish of the sea, the birds of the air, the [*tame*] beasts, and over all of the earth, and over everything that creeps upon the earth. (Genesis 1:26)

First Thessalonians 5:23 also tells us that we are a triune being.

> Now may the God of peace Himself sanctify you completely; and may your whole spirit, soul, and body be preserved blameless at the coming of our Lord Jesus Christ. (1 Thessalonians 5:23)

Below is my personal rendition of Genesis 1:26 and 1 Thessalonians 5:23 combined.

> God said, "Let us make man in Our image, to be a triune being, spirit, soul, and body, for We are Father, Son, and Holy Spirit. Let Us make man according to Our likeness, to reflect Our attributes and character so man can be in the earthly realm like what We are in the spiritual realm, and let them have complete authority and rule over the fish of the sea, the birds of the air, the beasts, and over all of the earth, and over everything that creeps upon the earth."

We are made in the image of our triune God. God is a three-part being: Father, Son, and Holy Spirit. We also are a three-part being: spirit, soul, and body, making us in God's image. We are in God's likeness, having the attributes and character of God. We are like God in that we use words to speak things into existence, we have authority on earth as God has authority in the spirit realm, we can choose, and we have free will. Man's ability to choose is not limited to choices that God would like a man to make. We have the freedom (free will) to choose against God's wishes. In the second chapter of Genesis, God showed man he had the freedom to choose other than what God wanted for man. Let's read Genesis 2:15–17.

> v. 15 Then the LORD God took the man and put him in the garden of Eden to tend and keep it.
>
> v. 16 And the LORD God commanded the man, saying, "Of every tree of the garden you may freely eat;
>
> v. 17 but of the tree of the knowledge of good and evil you shall not eat, for in the day that you eat of it you shall surely die." (Genesis 2:15–17)

In verses 16 and 17, God tells Adam that he had the option to eat fruit from every tree in the garden, but God also instructed Adam not to eat the fruit of the tree of the knowledge of good and evil. By giving Adam the option of eating or not eating from the tree of the knowledge of good and evil, God was showing Adam that he had the freedom to choose. Adam could choose what God wanted or what God didn't want.

We see Adam exercising his ability to choose in the first project God gave to Adam in Genesis 2:19–20.

> v. 19 Out of the ground the LORD God formed every beast of the field and every bird of the air, and brought *them* to Adam to see what he would call them. And whatever Adam called each living creature, that *was* its name.
>
> v. 20 So Adam gave names to all cattle, to the birds of the air, and to every beast of the field. But for Adam there was not found a helper comparable to him. (Genesis 2:19–20)

Selecting a name for every animal was making a lot of choices. Think about the city or town where you live. How many streets are in your town? If the mayor came to you and asked you to rename all the streets, you would have to make many choices. I think you would have to agree that Adam had to make numerous choices.

We all make a lot of choices each day. Sometimes we desire not to choose. Earlier I talked about Deuteronomy 30:19 being like a true-or-false test where God gives you the correct answer. When taking a true-or-false, multiple-choice, or fill-in-the-blank test, you might have found yourself pondering the answer to a question, but you couldn't decide (choose) an answer. So you decided to skip that question with the intention of returning to the question. But you forgot to go back and answer the question before turning in the test. I have done this exact thing. When I received the test back, the question I didn't respond to was marked incorrect. Here is the thing about this situation. Let's say it was a true-or-false question. So it seems that there are only two answers to pick. A third option to the question is to give no answer. Giving no response to the question is a response to the question. I give this example to show that not choosing is a choice. You chose not to answer. For example, in the United States, as in many other countries, if there is an election and if you choose not to vote, you have made a choice. You have chosen to have others decide for you. So if you say "I don't want to choose" or "I can't decide," you have chosen or decided. You know the old saying, "Indecision is a decision."

The fact that indecision is a decision is clearly shown in a person's salvation. I say that because people may think, *I will wait to give my life to Christ.* It is as though they are saying, "I will wait until I have thoroughly enjoyed the sin of this world before I decide to live for God." One of the problems with waiting is choosing to stay in their current condition, which is the path to hell. People's wonderful choice is to come into a personal relationship with God. We don't have to choose an eternity in hell because we are on that path. We get to choose eternity with God. We are all born on the hell or wrong side of the tracks. We all are given a free pass to eternity with God until we come of age and have an understanding of right and wrong. We have to choose to move to the other side of the tracks. Most people are comfortable with the side of the tracks they live on and don't move. God's desire is for men to move to His side of the tracks and receive salvation, as stated in 1 Timothy 2:3–4.

> For this *is* good and acceptable in the sight
> of God our Savior, who desires all men to be
> saved and to come to the knowledge of the truth.
> (1 Timothy 2:3–4)

God has even made choosing salvation as simple as shown in Romans 10:9–10 and Romans 10:13.

> That if you confess with your mouth the
> Lord Jesus and believe in your heart that God has
> raised Him from the dead, you will be saved. For

> with the heart one believes unto righteousness,
> and with the mouth confession is made unto sal-
> vation. (Romans 10:9–10)

and

> For "WHOEVER CALLS ON THE NAME OF THE
> LORD SHALL BE SAVED." (Romans 10:13)

God wants everyone saved, but each person must choose to accept the Lordship of Jesus. The second problem with waiting to choose a relationship with God is nobody knows the date or time when they will die. By choosing to wait, they have determined that they have time. But they don't know when something could happen that would end their life. Few people get the opportunity to receive salvation on their deathbed. Most people don't have the same good fortune as the men crucified with Jesus. Even then, knowing that they were about to die, only one chose eternal life with Jesus.

Some people think that they don't have a choice in what happens in their life. They believe God is in control of everything. If God controls everything, I agree that what you choose doesn't matter. However, God doesn't control everything. I talked about Adam and Eve eating the forbidden fruit. God didn't control their choices. I talked about salvation and how God desires all men to repent and receive salvation. But all men will not be saved because God gave man the ability to choose. God gave each of us individual free will through the ability to choose, and He will not usurp our free will. That is why God doesn't force men to be saved and why we can't force others to be saved.

God also gave man the authority to choose what happens on earth, as shown in Genesis 1:26–28.

> v. 26 Then God said, "Let Us make man in
> Our image, according to Our likeness; let them
> have dominion over the fish of the sea, over the
> birds of the air, and over the cattle, over all the

earth and over every creeping thing that creeps on the earth."

v. 27 So God created man in His *own* image; in the image of God He created him; male and female He created them.

v. 28 Then God blessed them, and God said to them, "Be fruitful and multiply; fill the earth and subdue it; have dominion over the fish of the sea, over the birds of the air, and over every living thing that moves on the earth." (Genesis 1:26–28)

Here we read that God gave man authority over the earth and over all fish, birds, and everything that lives on the earth. Because God gave man authority over the earth, He limited His authority over the earth. Every time in the Bible that God gives a promise, He limits His authority. People would attempt to prove that God couldn't do all things when I was growing up. They would ask, "Can God make a wall so high that He can't jump over?" Yes is the answer. If God made a wall with the intent that He would not be able to jump over the wall, He would not be able to jump over that wall. God just limited His jumping ability. Note that doesn't mean that He could not get to the other side of the wall. God could go under, through, or around the wall. God's Words are true, and He will not alter His Word. But the words we speak aren't always true. We might tell someone that we will meet them for lunch at a restaurant at noon on Monday. We get to the restaurant at 12:08 p.m. Our thought might be, *I am only eight minutes late. That is acceptable.* We didn't keep our word, making our word *not* the truth. God's Word is truth. If God says it, He will do it. Numbers 23:19 tells us that what God says will be done.

God *is* not a man, that He should lie, Nor a son of man, that He should repent. Has He said, and will He not do? Or has He spoken, and will He not make it good? (Numbers 23:19)

The verse states that God doesn't lie and doesn't have to repent from what He says. The verse also contrasts God's not being able to lie with man's ability to lie. I know that I have told a lie here and there. You may not have lied. You might have just stretched the truth from time to time. None of us have kept God's standard. The verse also tells us that whatever God says, He will do; and to make sure this point is clear, He states it a little differently by saying what He speaks will come to pass. Because God cannot lie, those things that He has spoken through men in the Bible and what He speaks through men today shall happen.

Consider the birth, death, and resurrection of Jesus. God spoke of Jesus, the things Jesus would perform, and the things He would suffer through the prophets. Jesus came into this world as prescribed and accomplished everything the prophets said He would. The point is that God is not controlling our individual choices. God controls the big picture through what He spoke in the beginning and through what He has spoken through man. When God speaks to us personally, it is primarily through His Word and the Holy Spirit. But that is guidance, not control. You are still able to choose. So make your choices—choices for life, because each of your choices matters.

CHAPTER 2

Your Choice Matters

With the ability to choose comes the ability to make good and bad choices. Whether our choices are good or bad, they affect our life and, most likely, someone else's life. So your choices do matter. Proverb 14:12 states how our choices can be a life-or-death choice.

There is a way *that seems* right to a man, But
its end *is* the way of death. (Proverbs 14:12)

The verse says there is a way. When I read the word *way*, I think about a road, path, or direction. The translator added the word *seems* to the verse to clarify the statement and talk about, in this verse, appearing to be correct. So this verse tells us that there is a choice of direction that we perceive is the right direction. But that choice of direction will lead to death because it only seems correct. But this same verse also means that there is a choice of direction that will lead to life. There is a correct road, path, or direction that, when chosen, leads to life. Because the choices you make matter to your life and the lives of others, I will discuss some choices in the Bible and what effects they had.

Adam and Eve

I said what you choose affects your life and others. Stop reading for a moment and think about your or someone else's choices that have affected your life more than anything else.

A great answer would be Adam and Eve eating the fruit from the tree of the knowledge of good and evil. That is one of the most important life-and-death decisions ever made by man. The other even more critical choice made was Jesus choosing to sacrifice His life on the cross for mankind. The account of the choice Adam and Eve made starts in Genesis 2:8 and goes through Genesis 3:6. Here are the scriptural highlights:

> v. 8 The Lord God planted a garden eastward in Eden, and there He put the man whom He had formed.
>
> v. 9 And out of the ground the Lord God made every tree grow that is pleasant to the sight and good for food. The tree of life *was* also in the midst of the garden, and the tree of the knowledge of good and evil. (Genesis 2:8–9)

Here we read that God made a garden, which in the midst was the tree of life (eternal fellowship with God) and the tree of the knowledge of good and evil. We will continue reading Genesis chapter 2.

> v. 15 Then the Lord God took the man and put him in the garden of Eden to tend and keep it.
>
> v. 16 And the Lord God commanded the man, saying, "Of every tree of the garden you may freely eat;
>
> v. 17 but of the tree of the knowledge of good and evil you shall not eat, for in the day

that you eat of it you shall surely die." (Genesis
2:15–17)

In Genesis 2:15–17, God put the man in the garden and told
the man that he could eat fruit from every tree except the tree of
the knowledge of good and evil, which would cause death (separation from God). Which gave Adam a choice of what trees he could
eat fruit from. Truly this is a choice between life and death, as in
Deuteronomy 30:19. In Genesis chapter 2, God set before all men
the choice of eating the fruit of the tree of life or eating the fruit
of the tree of the knowledge of good and evil because we all were
in Adam. God told Adam not to choose to eat from the tree of the
knowledge of good and evil, for it would cause death (spiritual separation from God).

Now we come to chapter 3 in Genesis. Adam now has Eve as
his mate. The devil tempted Eve to eat the fruit from the tree of the
knowledge of good and evil. Adam and Eve each make a life-altering
choice. These choices have affected all mankind for all our time on
this earth. Adam and Eve ate the fruit from the tree of the knowledge
of good and evil, as shown in Genesis 3:6.

> So when the woman saw that the tree *was*
> good for food, that it *was* pleasant to the eyes,
> and a tree desirable to make *one* wise, she took
> of its fruit and ate. She also gave to her husband
> with her, and he ate. (Genesis 3:6)

I can imagine Adam watching Eve eat the fruit from the tree of
the knowledge of good and evil (the forbidden fruit) and thinking,
She didn't die (bodily death). You might be thinking that God said
that if they ate the forbidden fruit, they would surely die a physical
death. We are a spirit that has a soul and lives in a body. The death
God was speaking of here is spiritual death, separation from Him.
Adam and Eve had an immediate spiritual death and, many years
later, physical death. Genesis 5:5 tells us that Adam lived for 930
years.

As we continue in Genesis chapter 3, we will explore what happened after Adam and Eve made these choices.

> v. 7 Then the eyes of both of them were opened, and they knew that they *were* naked; and they sewed fig leaves together and made themselves coverings.
> v. 8 And they heard the sound of the Lord God walking in the garden in the cool of the day, and Adam and his wife hid themselves from the presence of the Lord God among the trees of the garden.
> v. 9 Then the Lord God called to Adam and said to him, "Where *are* you?"
> v. 10 So he said, "I heard Your voice in the garden, and I was afraid because I was naked; and I hid myself." (Genesis 3:7–10)

The first thing verse 7 tells us is that the eyes of Adam and Eve were opened after they sinned. Obviously, Adam and Eve could see naturally. What was opened was the eyes of their understanding of good and evil. They now had an understanding of the difference between good and evil. Until then, they only knew good and were in unity with God. Because of their new knowledge, they knew that they were naked and attempted to cover themselves. Verses 8 and 9 tell us that God came to the garden to visit them. In verse 10, we discover that Adam and Eve hid from God, which was unlike their previous behavior. Also, we read that Adam told God that they hid because they were afraid. Before eating the forbidden fruit, they were never afraid of God. We will continue exploring Genesis 3 by looking at verses 16 through 19.

> v. 16 To the woman He said: "I will greatly multiply your sorrow and your conception; In pain you shall bring forth children; Your desire

shall be for your husband, And he shall rule over you."

v. 17 Then to Adam He said, "Because you have heeded the voice of your wife, and have eaten from the tree of which I commanded you, saying, 'You shall not eat of it': "Cursed *is* the ground for your sake; In toil you shall eat *of* it All the days of your life.

v. 18 Both thorns and thistles it shall bring forth for you, And you shall eat the herb of the field.

v. 19 In the sweat of your face you shall eat bread Till you return to the ground, For out of it you were taken; For dust you *are*, And to dust you shall return." (Genesis 3:16–19)

These verses describe God's actions toward Adam and Eve after eating the forbidden fruit. God said to Eve (representing all women) that He would multiply her sorrow and conception. He also told Eve that she would have pain during childbirth. Telling me that pain was not part of childbirth. Lastly, God told Eve that her desire would be for her husband and that he would rule over her.

The following three verses are God speaking to Adam (representing all men). God told Adam that He would curse the ground and it would take hard work to produce food for Eve and himself. That thorns and thistles would come from the ground. This means that there were no weeds up to that point in their lives and that tending the garden was not difficult. God also told Adam that they would eat from what he would grow and that the working of the garden would be hard enough to make him sweat. Lastly, God told Adam that he would become as the earth he came from when he physically died, which applies to both men and women.

Adam and Eve's sin affected us spiritually, and God's curses have affected the natural world. Luke 4:5–6 and Romans 16:6 reveal the worst thing about Adam and Eve eating the forbidden fruit.

> v. 5 Then the devil, taking Him up on a high mountain, showed Him all the kingdoms of the world in a moment of time.
>
> v. 6 And the devil said to Him, "All this authority I will give You, and their glory; for *this* has been delivered to me, and I give it to whomever I wish." (Luke 4:5–6)

These two verses come from when the devil tempted Jesus. In verse 6, the devil told Jesus that he was willing to give Jesus the authority of this world given to him by Adam. Adam received authority on the earth from God. Let's look at Romans 16:6 to see how Adam gave his authority to the devil.

> Do you not know that to whom you present yourselves slaves to obey, you are that one's slaves whom you obey, whether of sin *leading* to death, or of obedience *leading* to righteousness? (Romans 16:6)

Romans 16:6 informs us that whom you obey, you become their slave. Because Adam obeyed the devil, man became the servant of the devil, giving the devil Adam's authority. The slave owner owns all the possessions of the slave. We also know from 2 Corinthians 4:3–4 that the devil is the ruler of this world.

> v. 3 But even if our gospel is veiled, it is veiled to those who are perishing,
>
> v. 4 whose minds the god of this age has blinded, who do not believe, lest the light of the gospel of the glory of Christ, who is the image of God, should shine on them. (2 Corinthians 4:3–4)

Verse 4 indicates that the devil is the god of the world in this age. That the devil has blinded the thoughts of men so that they will not believe in Christ. To ensure that the light of the gospel of Christ wouldn't shine on their hearts. The light of Christ has shined on my heart, and hopefully, it has also shined on your heart. John 10:10 gives the problem with the devil having Adam's authority and being the ruler of the earth.

> The thief does not come except to steal, and to kill, and to destroy. I have come that they may have life, and that they may have *it* more abundantly. (John 10:10)

The thief in this verse is the devil, and his only desire with man is to steal, kill, and destroy. I thank God that there is a remedy for the sin that has infected man (due to the choices of Adam and Eve) and for the devil's desire to steal, kill, and destroy. That remedy is Jesus, Who came to give us abundant life.

Jesus

My choices have not impacted the lives of others as the choices of Adam and Eve. But my choices do have an impact. However, Jesus's choice has had a more significant impact on humans than the choice of any other man. Jesus was born, lived, and died so that man could live eternally with God. The Bible reveals this purpose in John 3:16–17.

> v. 16 For God so loved the world that He gave His only begotten Son, that whoever believes in Him should not perish but have everlasting life.
> v. 17 For God did not send His Son into the world to condemn the world, but that the world through Him might be saved. (John 3:16–17)

Jesus gave man the ability to choose to get back what Adam and Eve lost, everlasting fellowship with God, and the ability to resist the Devil's efforts to steal, kill and destroy. Jesus also gave man the ability to be redeemed from the curse of the law, as noted in Galatians 3:13.

> v. 13 Christ has redeemed us from the curse of the law, having become a curse for us (for it is written, "CURSED IS EVERYONE WHO HANGS ON A TREE"). (Galatians 3:13)

Because Jesus's seed didn't come through Adam but from God, Jesus was not a spiritually cursed human. Man's curse is transferred through the seed of a man. In Luke 1:35, the angel told Mary how she would conceive God's child. The angel said the Holy Spirit would come upon her and that the power of God would overshadow her and that the child would be called the Son of God. The seed that impregnated Mary was God's seed, His Word.

Jesus's death enabled man's redemption from the curse of the law. Deuteronomy 28:15–68 tells us what Jesus redeemed you from. However, Jesus in John 10:17–18 tells us that His death was a voluntary act.

> v. 17 Therefore My Father loves Me, because I lay down My life that I may take it again.
> v. 18 No one takes it from Me, but I lay it down of Myself. I have power to lay it down, and I have power to take it again. This command I have received from My Father. (John 10:17–18)

Jesus voluntarily laid down His life for you, me, and every person who ever lived on this earth. John 15:13 tells us that there is no greater love than to lay down your life for a friend. For how many of your friends would you lay down your life? Let's go a step further. For how many people whom you don't know would you sacrifice your life? Remember the two captured sailors in the movie *Midway*. One sailor gave up his life rather than divulging the location of the US ships. He gave his life for his friends and those that he didn't know. Jesus chose to suffer death on the cross so that all mankind might be saved. Isaiah 53:4–6 explains His suffering and what His suffering accomplished.

> v. 4 Surely He has borne our griefs (sicknesses, weaknesses, and distresses) and carried our sorrows *and* pains [*of punishment*], yet we [*ignorantly*] considered Him stricken, smitten, and afflicted by God [*as if with leprosy*]. [Matt. 8:17]
>
> v. 5 But He was wounded for our transgressions, He was bruised for our guilt *and* iniquities; the chastisement [*needful to obtain*] peace *and* well-being for us was upon Him, and with the stripes [*that wounded*] Him we are healed *and* made whole.
>
> v. 6 All we like sheep have gone astray, we have turned every one to his own way; and the Lord has made to light upon Him the guilt *and* iniquity of us all. [1 Pet. 2:24–25] (Isaiah 53:4–6 AMPC)

The choice Jesus made was not an easy decision to make or an easy choice to perform. Consider the stress Jesus faced, a man without the sin nature, in the garden of Gethsemane. We read about Jesus's struggle in the garden of Gethsemane in Matthew 26:36–46, Luke 22:39–46, and Mark 14:32–50. In Luke 22:41–44, we see the conflict between Jesus's human desire to live and His desire to fulfill what He came to accomplish on earth.

> v. 41 And He was withdrawn from them about a stone's throw, and He knelt down and prayed,

> v. 42 saying, "Father, if it is Your will, take this cup away from Me; nevertheless not My will, but Yours, be done."
>
> v. 43 Then an angel appeared to Him from heaven, strengthening Him.
>
> v. 44 And being in agony, He prayed more earnestly. Then His sweat became like great drops of blood falling down to the ground. (Luke 22:41–44)

Jesus was a man that had a will to live. In verse 42, He asked God to take away this divine appointment from Him. But His asking for the divine appointment to be removed was followed by Jesus's heart statement that God's will be done, not His own will. The choice Jesus made has affected my life and your life. His choice truly mattered, for it has affected all of mankind. It affected all those that lived before the death of Jesus and all those that lived after His death.

Jesus's choice to fulfill His purpose here on earth certainly has impacted my life. I chose to respond to the offer of eternal life and end my separation from God. That is, I accepted Jesus as my Lord and Savior. My salvation was that I chose to believe in my heart that Jesus is the son of God, and I chose to confess out loud that Jesus is my Lord. That sounds a lot like Romans 10:9–10.

> v. 9 that if you confess with your mouth the Lord Jesus and believe in your heart that God has raised Him from the dead, you will be saved.
>
> v. 10 For with the heart one believes unto righteousness, and with the mouth confession is made unto salvation. (Romans 10:9–10)

I think I always believed in Jesus, but I didn't understand about being a Christian. Nor was I ready, before this time, to become a Christian. But I changed my mind. That is what it takes to choose a life with Jesus: a change of mind.

My mind changed one day when I was reflecting on my life. My life was not going as I thought it should be going. I was divorced, something that I never thought would happen to me. I had a child from that marriage, which was the best thing that came out of that relationship. I found myself in and out of meaningless relationships. To make the whole situation worse, I discovered that I didn't have a purpose for my life.

My thought process at that time in my life was that life was similar to a game. You know what comes with every game you buy. Yes, the rules for the game. I changed when I figured God designed this game, so I should follow God's rules. I considered God's rule book to be the Bible. So I chose to start going to church to learn more about the Bible. It took a while of going to church and reading the Bible before I gave my life to Christ.

The choice to become a believer in Jesus did matter. I regained my purpose in life. I married Annette, my beautiful wife, a believer I met at church. I was able to raise my daughter from my first marriage for a couple of years and Annette's son from her first marriage. Annette and I adopted a baby girl, and about seven years later, we adopted a five-year boy. I believe that Annette and I made a difference in our adopted daughter's life, who now has beautiful twin girls. We wanted to make a difference in the life of the little boy we adopted, but he never chose to become part of our family. Our other son has his own family, which also includes twin girls and three other children. As for the little boy we adopted, we discovered that you and I might desire to help someone, but they have to choose to let you help them. People make their own life choices.

I say that your choices matter because if I would not choose to follow after Jesus, I don't think those other wonderful things would have happened. My life in the natural was not terrible. But it was on a path that only seemed good. I am not saying that I have been perfect after becoming a believer because I have not. But even though I have made some wrong choices, my heart desires to choose the plan that God has for me. I am truly thankful for Jesus and His choosing to sacrifice His life so that you and I could have eternal life.

Sowing and Reaping

My wife likes to grow fruits and vegetables; however, we don't have the room for a big garden where we now live. So she has planters, some large pots, and hydroponic systems. Recently she planted some potatoes. One day Annette pointed out some green leafy stems and said, "Look at my potatoes." She didn't say, "I wonder what is growing in that pot." She knew what was growing because that is what she planted. She chose to plant (sow) potatoes because she wanted to harvest (reap) potatoes. Everyone understands this process when it comes to growing food, but we tend to lose sight of it for the rest of our lives.

Have you ever, while driving, known that someone wanted to get over into your lane, and you didn't let them over? Then the next day or week or month later, you need to get over into another lane, and they would not let you over. Did you get a little upset with them, or did you think you just reaped what you sowed? Galatians 6:7 says,

> Do not be deceived, God is not mocked;
> for whatever a man sows, that he will also reap.
> (Genesis 6:7)

This verse tells us that we will reap corn if we sow corn seeds. Don't deceive yourself into thinking that you can sow corn and reap wheat. This verse indicates that you will reap what you have sown. For example, when you sow corn seeds, you don't wake up the next day and harvest corn. When you plant corn, first you get a stalk, then the ears of corn, and after the ears, you receive the whole corn in the ear. Understanding this process is extremely important, as noted by Jesus in Mark 4:13.

> And He said to them, "Do you not understand this parable? How then will you understand all the parables?" (Mark 4:13)

As believers in Jesus, we need a complete understanding of the process of sowing and reaping because we are constantly sowing. Ministers tell us that we need to give money to receive more money when we are in financial need. Just as in the example of sowing corn, money does not just appear when sowing money. God could have someone give us money. God may give us an idea of a way to earn more money, or maybe we will receive a promotion to provide us with more money. We need to hear instructions from God as to what to do and not just assume money will drop out of the sky.

The sowing and reaping process also means we will not sow evil and reap good, as Proverbs 22:8 tells us.

> He who sows iniquity will reap calamity
> *and* futility, and the rod of his wrath [*with which*
> *he smites others*] will fail. (Proverbs 22:8 AMPC)

The verse informs us that you will reap calamity and futility when sowing iniquity, or should I say evil. The King James Bible calls *calamity* and *futility* "sorrow." The calamity, futility, or sorrow are reaped as the results of the iniquity or evil that was sown.

Another result of sowing and reaping is in 2 Corinthians.

> But this *I say:* He who sows sparingly will
> also reap sparingly, and he who sows bountifully
> will also reap bountifully. (2 Corinthians 9:6)

This verse is exciting. You get to choose what you reap and also the amount of the harvest. If you choose to sow a little corn, you will reap a little corn. But if you sow a lot of corn, you will reap a lot of corn. The process of sowing and reaping will always be there, as stated in Genesis 8:22.

> While the earth remains, Seedtime and har-
> vest, Cold and heat, Winter and summer, And
> day and night Shall not cease. (Genesis 8:22)

The verse tells us that there will always be a time for sowing and harvesting. That means a time to plant seeds and a time for harvesting will always exist. An interesting aspect of harvesting is that all plants aren't ready for harvesting on the same timetable. Corn takes 55 to 95 days to grow before harvesting. Wheat takes 110 to 130 days from planting to harvest. When planting an apple seed, it can take 7 to 10 years before you can harvest apples. It tells us that when we plant a seed, the time for harvest will depend on what type of seed we plant. Some seeds have an immediate harvest, while other seeds take years before we receive a harvest. In life, we plant seeds that we don't know the time for harvest, so we should continue to water the plant until harvest. Galatians 6:9 tells us not to give up on what we have planted.

> And let us not grow weary while doing good, for in due season we shall reap if we do not lose heart. (Genesis 6:9)

Every good gardener knows that you need to tend to the garden. You have to make sure you water and remove weeds from the garden. This verse tells us there will be a harvesttime as long as we don't destroy or give up on what we have sown.

Our lives are like a garden. Our words and actions are the seeds we sow into our life garden. Mark 4:14 says that the sower sows the word. Here *the word* is referred to as seeds that are sown. Proverbs 18:21 talks about the words we speak.

> Death and life *are* in the power of the tongue, And those who love it will eat its fruit. (Proverbs 18:21)

Our words have the power to create death or life in us and others. We need to choose to speak life. In Numbers 13 and 14, God told Moses to send twelve spies into the land He had given them. When the spies came back, ten of the spies chose to give what God called an evil report. It sounds like they sowed some evil seeds. Two of the spies chose to give a good report. That sounds like they sowed good seeds. The adult people in the congregation agreed with the evil seeds that were spoken. What was reaped? The people giving the evil report and those that agreed with the evil report died over the next forty years while traveling in the wilderness. Joshua and Caleb, who gave the good report, reaped the promised land and were the only two in their generation to enter the promised land.

We must understand that we are constantly sowing with our words and the things we do. We sow love and hate, forgiveness and unforgiveness, kindness and meanness, prosperity and lack with the words we speak and the things we do. God sowed the entire universe through spoken words in the first chapter of Genesis. Let's look at the number of times in Genesis 1 that it says "God said" while He was creating the things of this world.

> Then <u>God said</u>, "Let there be light"; and there was light. (Genesis 1:3)
>
> Then <u>God said</u>, "Let there be a firmament in the midst of the waters, and let it divide the waters from the waters." (Genesis 1:6)
>
> Then <u>God said</u>, "Let the waters under the heavens be gathered together into one place, and let the dry *land* appear"; and it was so. (Genesis 1:9)
>
> Then <u>God said</u>, "Let the earth bring forth grass, the herb *that* yields seed, *and* the fruit tree *that* yields fruit according to its kind, whose seed *is* in itself, on the earth"; and it was so. (Genesis 1:11)
>
> Then <u>God said</u>, "Let there be lights in the firmament of the heavens to divide the day from the night; and let them be for signs and seasons, and for days and years. (Genesis 1:14)
>
> Then <u>God said</u>, "Let the waters abound with an abundance of living creatures, and let

birds fly above the earth across the face of the firmament of the heavens." (Genesis 1:20)

Then <u>God said</u>, "Let the earth bring forth the living creature according to its kind: cattle and creeping thing and beast of the earth, *each* according to its kind"; and it was so. (Genesis 1:24)

Then <u>God said</u>, "Let Us make man in Our image, according to Our likeness; let them have dominion over the fish of the sea, over the birds of the air, and over the cattle, over all the earth and over every creeping thing that creeps on the earth." (Genesis 1:26, underscores mine)

God, through His spoken words, created this world. As we read in Genesis 1:26, God created us (man) in His image and likeness, which gave us the creative power of the spoken word. Jesus, in Matthew 12:36, warns us about what we say.

But I say to you that for every idle word men may speak, they will give account of it in the day of judgment. (Matthew 12:36)

Here the word *idle* is speaking of evil words. Words that don't reflect God are evil. James chapter 3 talks about the tongue. The chapter tells how the tongue is powerful but almost impossible to control. Verses 8–10 are an example of how we speak both good and evil out of our mouths.

v. 8 But no man can tame the tongue. *It is* an unruly evil, full of deadly poison.

v. 9 With it we bless our God and Father, and with it we curse men, who have been made in the similitude of God.

> v. 10 Out of the same mouth proceed bless-
> ing and cursing. My brethren, these things ought
> not to be so. (James 3:8–10)

You can see that we sow words that bless us and bless others, but we also sow words that curse ourselves and others. We all desire our life garden to be pleasant and successful, so we must sow words and action that give us the harvest we desire. What do you want to reap?

Follow Me

Would you have liked an opportunity to become one of the inner circle of Jesus? I know of six people to whom Jesus directly said to them, "Follow Me," and four of them became part of His inner circle. There were others that Jesus called that became part of His inner circle, but the call, in Scripture, was not as direct as these six. Let's look at the response of these six called directly by Jesus. First, I will discuss the disciples who responded by following Jesus.

> v. 18 And Jesus, walking by the sea of
> Galilee, saw two brethren, Simon called Peter,
> and Andrew his brother, casting a net into the
> sea: for they were fishers.
> v. 19 And he saith unto them, Follow me,
> and I will make you fishers of men.
> v. 20 And they straightway left *their* nets,
> and followed him. (Matthew 4:18–20)

Another person that Jesus called in this manner was the disciple Matthew, sometimes called Levi.

> And as Jesus passed forth from thence, he
> saw a man, named Matthew, sitting at the receipt
> of custom: and he saith unto him, Follow me.
> And he arose, and followed him. (Matthew 9:9)

Then there is Philip, whom Jesus called to follow Him in John 1:43.

> The following day Jesus wanted to go to
> Galilee, and He found Philip and said to him,
> "Follow Me." (John 1:43)

In these verses, Peter's, Andrew's, and Matthew's responses were immediately to follow after Jesus. The Bible doesn't say that Philip's response was to follow Jesus immediately. John 1:45 tells us something about Philip's response.

> Philip found Nathanael and said to him,
> "We have found Him of whom Moses in the law,
> and also the prophets, wrote—Jesus of Nazareth,
> the son of Joseph." (John 1:45)

I see Philip's response as saying, "Yes, I will follow You, but let me quickly go and find my good friend Nathanael because he will want to follow You also." Philip was ready to follow Jesus immediately, but his love for his friend caused him to find Nathanael first.

When Jesus calls, your response should be to obey and follow Him no matter who you are. So let's look at the fifth person that Jesus said to follow Him in chapter 8 of Matthew.

> v. 21 Then another of His disciples said to
> Him, "Lord, let me first go and bury my father."
> v. 22 But Jesus said to him, "Follow Me,
> and let the dead bury their own dead." (Matthew
> 8:21–22)

I am going to call this person the other disciple. As you can see, this person was already a disciple, and he just wasn't one of the disciples that traveled with Jesus. Jesus had twelve disciples that were close to Him. But He had many more disciples than the Twelve. It appears that the other disciple also wanted to, at some point, travel with Jesus. What is interesting about the other disciple is that he wanted to bury his father first. Your thought might be, *That doesn't sound terrible.* He wanted to bury his father. Some believe his father was only sick or very old. If that is the case, what the other disciple was saying was, "I will follow You after my father dies and I get my inheritance." The main point is that he gave a selfish excuse for not immediately following Jesus.

I know that I have given excuses for not immediately following Jesus. You probably have never had the Holy Spirit lead you to do something and didn't promptly obey. I know I have. The scripture doesn't tell us if the other disciple followed or not. However, Jesus's response of "Follow me; and let the dead bury their dead" is thought-provoking. I believe that Jesus is telling the other disciple that "those not following Me are dead. The dead should bury their own, but if you are following after Me, you have found life and should stay with the living." The other disciple most likely chose to stay with his family because it was inconvenient to leave them at that time.

Let's take a look at the sixth person in this "Follow Me" group.

> v. 16 Now behold, one came and said to Him, "Good Teacher, what good thing shall I do that I may have eternal life?"
>
> v. 17 So He said to him, "Why do you call Me good? No one *is* good but One, *that is,* God. But if you want to enter into life, keep the commandments."
>
> v. 18 He said to Him, "Which ones?" Jesus said, "'YOU SHALL NOT MURDER,' 'YOU SHALL NOT COMMIT ADULTERY,' 'YOU SHALL NOT STEAL,' 'YOU SHALL NOT BEAR FALSE WITNESS,'
>
> v. 19 'HONOR YOUR FATHER AND YOUR MOTHER,' and, 'YOU SHALL LOVE YOUR NEIGHBOR AS YOURSELF.'"

> v. 20 The young man said to Him, "All these things I have kept from my youth. What do I still lack?"
>
> v. 21 Jesus said to him, "If you want to be perfect, go, sell what you have and give to the poor, and you will have treasure in heaven; and come, follow Me."
>
> v. 22 But when the young man heard that saying, he went away sorrowful, for he had great possessions. (Matthew 19:16–22)

I am going to call this person the rich young man. The first difference between the rich young man and the four who followed after Jesus is in verse 16. The rich young man came to Jesus. He sought out Jesus where Jesus came to Peter, Andrew, Matthew, and Philip. The other disciple was already with Jesus. The rich young man didn't ask to follow or travel with Jesus. He wanted to know what he must do to inherit eternal life. That sounds like something everyone would desire to learn. In verse 17, Jesus informs the rich young man that he must keep the commandments to have eternal life. He then asks Jesus in verse 18, "Which ones?" An interesting question after being told, "Keep the commandments." Implied in the answer of "Keep the commandments" is to keep all of the commandments. In verse 19, Jesus is gracious and gives the rich young man a few commandments. He answers Jesus in verse 20, saying, "All these things I have kept from my youth." The problem with the rich young man's answer is that he is saying that by following these few commandments, he had been righteous. He thought that through his works, he could be righteous. The law's purpose was to show that no one on their own can be righteous. Because only one man, Jesus, fulfilled the whole law. Jesus tells the rich young man what he needs to do to be perfect. He gives the rich young man instructions on what he must do to have treasures in heaven and tells him to "follow Me." The rich young man's response to "follow Me" is entirely different from Peter's, Andrew's, Matthew's, and Philip's responses but most likely the same as the other disciple's response. He becomes sad and leaves Jesus. Verse 22 also says that he didn't follow Jesus because he had great possessions. Actually, his possessions had him.

It is always easier to join a cause after it is popular. The other disciple and the rich young man knew the popularity of Jesus's ministry and the miracles performed by Jesus. Yet when called to have a deeper relationship with Jesus, they didn't because the things of this world had a hold on them. The following of Jesus by Peter, Andrew, Matthew, and Philip was a significant act of faith because they left all to follow Jesus at the beginning of His ministry.

If you don't choose to obey Jesus, you will never know how that response could change your life. For example, in Acts 1:26, they drew lots, and Matthias became one of the twelve apostles. If the other disciple or the rich young man had followed Jesus, perhaps one of them would have been chosen as an apostle. But neither one of them chose to follow Jesus. In Mark 10:29–30, Jesus told Peter what would happen to those that left all to follow Him

> v. 29 So Jesus answered and said, "Assuredly, I say to you, there is no one who has left house or brothers or sisters or father or mother or wife or children or lands, for My sake and the gospel's,
> v. 30 who shall not receive a hundredfold now in this time—houses and brothers and sisters and mothers and children and lands, with persecutions—and in the age to come, eternal life." (Mark 10:29–30)

These two verses tell us that the other disciple and the rich young man had nothing to lose but all to gain. Just as they had all to gain if they would have chosen to follow Jesus, you and I have all to gain by choosing to follow Jesus. I am not speaking about just becoming born-again but about becoming a true disciple of Jesus. Throughout the day, the Holy Spirit guides us in God's plan for our lives. We should all adhere to the example of Peter, Andrew, Matthew, and Philip and quickly follow the instructions of the Holy Spirit. The choices of these six men had a tremendous effect on their lives and our lives. The other disciple and the rich young man chose not to follow Jesus, keeping one foot in the path of this world, and were not mentioned again. Always respond immediately to any request or command from Jesus, whether from His Word or the Holy Spirit.

CHAPTER 3

Old Testament Choices

The choices people make in the Bible can be divided into two categories. They are choices that show trust in God or choices that show trust in the things of this world. In this and the next chapter, I will discuss a few choices made in the Old Testament and the New Testament of the Bible. In my reading of the Bible, I noticed that the primary individuals in the numerous accounts in the Bible were people that, at some point, chose to believe and obey God. Some of these individuals chose to obey God and then chose to turn their back on God and disobey Him. At other times, the primary individuals in the account had no belief in the true God and then chose to believe in God and obey Him. In reading the Bible, you will find many scenarios of choosing belief or unbelief in God and choosing obedience or disobedience to God. The accounts of the Bible also show the many facets of man's relationship with God. God is the same yesterday, today, and forever. Man, however, is constantly in flux, choosing to believe God at one time and in a moment, choosing not to believe God. Choices in the accounts discussed in these two chapters are a few choices made in the Bible. The discussion of these choices should give revelation into the situations you find yourself in and what you should choose. This chapter will discuss some fascinating choices made in the Old Testament.

Noah

I will start the discussion with one man against the rest of the world. That man was Noah. Think of what it would be like to be in a situation where everyone else in the world is calling black *white*, and you are calling black what it is, black. That is similar to Noah's situation. Genesis chapter 6 tells of the condition in which God had found the earth.

> v. 5 Then the LORD saw that the wickedness of man *was* great in the earth, and *that* every intent of the thoughts of his heart *was* only evil continually.
>
> v. 6 And the LORD was sorry that He had made man on the earth, and He was grieved in His heart.
>
> v. 7 So the LORD said, "I will destroy man whom I have created from the face of the earth, both man and beast, creeping thing and birds of the air, for I am sorry that I have made them."
>
> v. 8 But Noah found grace in the eyes of the LORD.
>
> v. 9 This is the genealogy of Noah. Noah was a just man, perfect in his generations. Noah walked with God. (Genesis 6:5–9)

In verses 5–8, God informs us that He found great sin on the earth and that His response to what He found would be to destroy all flesh on the earth. But we are also told that Noah found grace with God. Genesis 6:9 tells us that Noah walked with God. Enoch is the only other person that the Bible says walked with God. Noah's walking with God tells us that Noah had chosen to have an extremely close relationship with God. Remember, God looked at man and had found only wickedness, except for Noah. God did not say that He found favor with Noah and his family, which tells me that the others in Noah's family didn't have Noah's relationship with God.

There must have been family pressure and pressure from everyone else around Noah attempting to conform him to the world's ways. God chose to save Noah because Noah chose to resist the pressure of sin and walk with Him. Here is what Genesis 6:13–18 says.

> v. 13 And God said to Noah, "The end of all flesh has come before Me, for the earth is filled with violence through them; and behold, I will destroy them with the earth.
>
> v. 14 Make yourself an ark of gopherwood; make rooms in the ark, and cover it inside and outside with pitch.
>
> v. 15 And this is how you shall make it: The length of the ark *shall be* three hundred cubits, its width fifty cubits, and its height thirty cubits.
>
> v. 16 You shall make a window for the ark, and you shall finish it to a cubit from above; and set the door of the ark in its side. You shall make it *with* lower, second, and third *decks*.
>
> v. 17 And behold, I Myself am bringing floodwaters on the earth, to destroy from under heaven all flesh in which *is* the breath of life; everything that *is* on the earth shall die.
>
> v. 18 But I will establish My covenant with you; and you shall go into the ark—you, your sons, your wife, and your sons' wives with you."
> (Genesis 6:13–18)

In verse 13, God tells Noah that He will destroy the earth. In verses 14–16, God gives Noah instructions on how to build the ark. The verses don't tell us if Noah had ever built a boat. In verse 17, God informs Noah how the earth would be destroyed. Up to this time, it had never rained, so Noah was most likely thinking, *What is rain, and what is a flood?* There is nothing that tells us whether boats did or didn't exist at that time. It is awesome how Noah trusted God and obeyed God. Think of the instructions given to Noah on how to build the ark. I compare the instruction given to Noah similar to waking up one day and having the designs on how to build a flux capacitor to travel back in time. Not only has a flux capacitor not been invented, nobody has ever traveled back in time. We know that Noah chose to obey and build the ark because, in Genesis 6:22, we are told that Noah did everything that God had commanded.

Noah's choice to do all that God commanded could only come from his close relationship with God. Through walking with God, Noah learned to trust God. How else do you build something you have never thought about to prepare for something that has never happened before? How would you respond to being told to prepare for something that had never occurred? Noah had never seen rain or a flood, but he prepared at God's command. We are to prepare for the return of Jesus. Have you prepared? In Noah's time, the earth had been watered by a mist that came up from the earth, yet Noah prepared for a flood. Noah chose to believe God, for something he had not seen. He didn't know what would happen, but he chose to trust God that something would happen.

We need to have Noah's kind of trust in God. God knows the end from the beginning. Therefore, when God tells us to do something, we need to trust that God knows what is happening and obey Him.

The 12 Spies

My favorite account about choosing to believe in God is the account of the twelve spies. Before the account of the twelve spies were the ten plagues, Moses leading the children of Israel out of Egypt, and Moses bringing God's people to the Red Sea. God parted the Red Sea, and the children of Israel crossed over on dry land. When the army of Egypt followed after the children of Israel, the Red Sea closed on them, killing Egypt's army. These miracles were just the beginning of the miracles God performed for His people. In Numbers, chapters 13 and 14, we come to the account of the twelve spies. The account starts with the Lord telling Moses to send one leader from each of the twelve tribes to spy out the land of Canaan, for God said that He had given them the land. Here is what the scriptures say about the twelve spies in the book of Numbers.

> v. 1 And the LORD spoke to Moses, saying,
> v. 2 "Send men to spy out the land of Canaan, which I am giving to the children of Israel; from each tribe of their fathers you shall send a man, every one a leader among them."
> (Numbers 13:1–2)

In Numbers 13:17–21, Moses chooses the twelve spies and sends them into the land. Like any commander, Moses tells the spies which way to go and to check on the strength of the people, what type of land it is, what kind of defense they have, and to bring some of the fruit (spoils) back. So they went to spy out the land. This account becomes even more interesting, starting with Numbers 13:25.

> v. 25 And they returned from spying out the land after forty days.
> v. 26 Now they departed and came back to Moses and Aaron and all the congregation of the children of Israel in the Wilderness of Paran, at Kadesh; they brought back word to them and to all the congregation, and showed them the fruit of the land.
> v. 27 Then they told him, and said: "We went to the land where you sent us. It truly flows with milk and honey, and this *is* its fruit.
> v. 28 Nevertheless the people who dwell in the land *are* strong; the cities *are* fortified *and* very large; moreover we saw the descendants of Anak there.
> v. 29 The Amalekites dwell in the land of the South; the Hittites, the Jebusites, and the Amorites dwell in the mountains; and the

Canaanites dwell by the sea and along the banks of the Jordan."

v. 30 Then Caleb quieted the people before Moses, and said, "Let us go up at once and take possession, for we are well able to overcome it."

v. 31 But the men who had gone up with him said, "We are not able to go up against the people, for they *are* stronger than we."

v. 32 And they gave the children of Israel a bad report of the land which they had spied out, saying, "The land through which we have gone as spies *is* a land that devours its inhabitants, and all the people whom we saw in it *are* men of *great* stature.

v. 33 There we saw the giants (the descendants of Anak came from the giants); and we were like grasshoppers in our own sight, and so we were in their sight." (Numbers 13:25–33)

These verses tell us that the spies returned, and ten spies chose to give a bad or negative report on the land. The report was bad because they chose to see the situation through their natural eyes and not God's eyes. Verse 30 tells us that Caleb chose to see the situation from God's eyes. Caleb said that the children of Israel were able to overcome the land's inhabitants.

Before we look harshly at the ten spies that chose not to trust God, consider the situations you have encountered. You know those situations where you wanted to believe in God, but in the natural, you couldn't see how to accomplish it. The problem that God's people had was their mindset. They were enslaved for over four hundred years, and even though Moses had delivered them from slavery in Egypt, mentally, they were still enslaved. Before you surrender your life to the lordship of Jesus, you are a slave to sin. Because we have to become mentally free, God tells us that we have to choose to renew our minds after we are born-again. The renewing of our minds allows us to choose God's way, and we start thinking God's thoughts. That is what happened to Noah. As Noah walked with God, he began to think like God. He didn't behave like the rest of the world because he didn't think like the rest of the world. His thoughts were God's thoughts. It's like being married. After being married and walking with your mate for a long time, you start finishing each other's sentences, or you know just what the other person is thinking. You will find in Numbers 14:6–10 that two spies gave a good report. They chose to put their trust in God.

> v. 6 But Joshua the son of Nun and Caleb the son of Jephunneh, *who were* among those who had spied out the land, tore their clothes;
>
> v. 7 and they spoke to all the congregation of the children of Israel, saying: "The land we passed through to spy out *is* an exceedingly good land.
>
> v. 8 If the LORD delights in us, then He will bring us into this land and give it to us, 'a land which flows with milk and honey.'
>
> v. 9 Only do not rebel against the LORD, nor fear the people of the land, for they *are* our bread; their protection has departed from them, and the LORD *is* with us. Do not fear them."
>
> v. 10 And all the congregation said to stone them with stones. Now the glory of the LORD appeared in the tabernacle of meeting before all the children of Israel. (Numbers 14:6–10)

Joshua and Caleb knew from all the people's experiences in leaving Egypt and their wilderness journey to the promised land that God was with them. God had told them He was giving them the land, and Joshua and Caleb chose to trust that just as God had delivered the people out of Egypt, He would bring them into the promised land. However, the people chose to believe the ten spies with the bad report. Now Joshua and Caleb, because of their choice to trust God, we're not just in opposition to the other ten leaders, but they were in opposition to all the people. In verse 10, the people were about to stone Joshua and Caleb, but the Lord intervened and stopped the people. However, because of the people's choice, we find out later in Numbers 14, verse 30 that of the adults, Caleb and Joshua were the only two to enter the promised land.

I said that this was my favorite account about choice. That is because it shows that if you are going contrary to a group of ten or all those around you, you have made the correct choice if you choose God's way.

Moses

The account of Moses is a wonderful account about you choosing who you are. Moses's life was greatly affected by the choices made for him. For example, Moses's mother chose not to kill him. Pharaoh's daughter chose to raise him. A decision not mentioned in the Bible is Pharaoh choosing to allow his daughter to raise the child. Think about the circumstances. Pharaoh and his daughter had to know that the child was a Hebrew boy. Then there are the choices that Moses made that affected his life. Those choices were born out of how Moses defined himself in the second chapter of Exodus.

> v. 11 Now it came to pass in those days, when Moses was grown, that he went out to his brethren and looked at their burdens. And he saw an Egyptian beating a Hebrew, one of his brethren.

> v. 12 So he looked this way and that way, and when he saw no one, he killed the Egyptian and hid him in the sand.

> v. 13 And when he went out the second day, behold, two Hebrew men were fighting, and he said to the one who did the wrong, "Why are you striking your companion?"

> v. 14 Then he said, "Who made you a prince and a judge over us? Do you intend to kill me as you killed the Egyptian?" So Moses feared and said, "Surely this thing is known!"
>
> v. 15 When Pharaoh heard of this matter, he sought to kill Moses. But Moses fled from the face of Pharaoh and dwelt in the land of Midian; and he sat down by a well. (Exodus 2:11–15)

Here we find in verse 11 that Moses knew that the Hebrews were his people because the verse said that he went out to his brethren. I am sure that Moses learned that he was a Hebrew from his birth family when his mother was nursing him for Pharaoh's daughter. Moses might have also heard stories of how Pharaoh's daughter found him in the river. Either way, Moses knew he was a Hebrew. In verses 12–15, we are shown an extreme action Moses took. Clarity into why Moses killed that Egyptian is in Acts 7:23–25.

> v. 23 Now when he was forty years old, it came into his heart to visit his brethren, the children of Israel.
>
> v. 24 And seeing one of *them* suffer wrong, he defended and avenged him who was oppressed, and struck down the Egyptian.
>
> v. 25 For he supposed that his brethren would have understood that God would deliver them by his hand, but they did not understand. (Acts 7:23–25)

Verse 23 lets us know that Moses was a grown man when he went to "visit his brethren." In verse 24, we're told that Moses killed an Egyptian for wrongfully treating a Hebrew. And in verse 25, we discover what Moses believed when he killed the Egyptian. Moses thought that God would use him to deliver the Hebrew people out of slavery and from the Egyptians. But Moses also believed that his brethren understood that God would use him to deliver them.

Because of this belief, Moses chose not to partake of the royalty's rich and luxurious life and rather to endure the harsh life with God's people, as Hebrews 11:24–26 says.

> v. 24 By faith Moses, when he became of age, refused to be called the son of Pharaoh's daughter,
> v. 25 choosing rather to suffer affliction with the people of God than to enjoy the passing pleasures of sin,
> v. 26 esteeming the reproach of Christ greater riches than the treasures in Egypt; for he looked to the reward. (Hebrews 11:24–26)

These verses tell us that Moses acted in faith. Faith is the corresponding action for what you hope for or in which you believe. The action in these verses was Moses refusing to be called the son of Pharaoh's daughter. By choosing not to be the son of Pharaoh's daughter, Moses chose to suffer as the people of God were. Moses knew that he was a Hebrew in his early years even though Pharaoh's daughter adopted him. It took faith walking out the belief that he was to deliver his people. It wouldn't be easy for any of us to be living the life of royalty in the greatest country at that time and reject that privilege and serve as the leader of slaves.

There are modern life examples of people giving up what the world would call success or being on top of the world to serve. One example that comes to mind for me is Pat Tillman, a pro football player. Many people would consider being a starter in professional football as being on top of the world. After the September 11 attack here in the United States, Pat left the NFL and joined the US Army. While in the Army, Pat became an Army Ranger. Pat chose to join the Army because of his loyalty to the United States. Later he died in action. What would you give up because of the importance of someone else or something else? Our salvation is due to Jesus leaving the best place ever created, heaven, and coming to earth to become the ransom payment for us.

Naaman

Naaman shows how a person can have the wrong mindset and then repent, obey God, and receive their miracle. This account of Naaman is in 2 Kings 5. As the Bible tells us, Naaman was the commander of the king of Syria's army. He was a man of valor, but he also was a leper. A young girl captured from the land of Israel was a servant to Naaman's wife. The servant girl told Naaman's wife that there was a prophet in Samaria that could heal Naaman's leprosy. Naaman, wanting his healing from leprosy, went to the king of Syria and told the king what the servant girl had said. Knowing how valuable Naaman was to him, the king told Naaman to go immediately. So Naaman went to Israel to find the prophet. But first, he had to go to the king of Israel. Elisha sent word to the king of Israel to send Naaman to him. This way, Naaman would know that there was a prophet in Israel. We read in 2 Kings 5:9–14 about the choices that Naaman made.

> v. 9 Then Naaman went with his horses and chariot, and he stood at the door of Elisha's house.
>
> v. 10 And Elisha sent a messenger to him, saying, "Go and wash in the Jordan seven times, and your flesh shall be restored to you, and *you shall* be clean."
>
> v. 11 But Naaman became furious, and went away and said, "Indeed, I said to myself, 'He will surely come out *to me,* and stand and call on the name of the Lord his God, and wave his hand over the place, and heal the leprosy.'" (2 Kings 5:9–11)

Here in verse 11, Naaman chooses to become angry. I believe Naaman was angry because, as we read in verse 10, Naaman couldn't believe that the man of God sent a servant to instruct him on receiving his healing, even though it was because of a servant that he was there. Naaman was insulted. He was a great general and had traveled a long distance to be healed by the man of God. Naaman's statement of "Indeed, I said to myself" tells us of his expectations of how he envisioned Elisha would heal him. People imagine how God will heal them, prosper them, and bless them. It is crucial to choose to be open to whatever God's plan is for your life. You don't know what process God will employ. It could be the man of God, as Naaman was expecting, or a servant with a message. But we should never choose to become offended because God acts in a way other than what we were expecting. Let's read on to understand the thoughts of Naaman.

> "Are not the Abanah and the Pharpar, the rivers of Damascus, better than all the waters of Israel? Could I not wash in them and be clean?" So he turned and went away in a rage. (2 Kings 5:12)

In this verse, we see that Naaman has chosen to question where he should wash. He wanted a cleaner river in which to wash. The idea of a man of his status washing in the dirty water of the Jordan was unacceptable to him. Let's read verses 13 and 14:

> v. 13 And his servants came near and spoke to him, and said, "My father, *if* the prophet had told you *to do* something great, would you not have done *it?* How much more then, when he says to you, 'Wash, and be clean'?"
> v. 14 So he went down and dipped seven times in the Jordan, according to the saying of the man of God; and his flesh was restored like the flesh of a little child, and he was clean. (2 Kings 5:13–14)

It is good to have someone in your life who can give you perspective, even a servant. Naaman listened to his servant and chose to follow the instructions of Elisha, and received his healing. I like this story because I see myself and others in Naaman. Do you see you? Hopefully, you will appreciate this example. I got out of my car at a shopping center, and while walking to the entrance, I saw this woman walking with a limp, and I heard God tell me to pray for her. I chose to obey God. My thought was, *I had heard God say to pray for this woman. Surely God is going to heal her.*

I asked if I could pray for her, and she began asking one question after another to determine if I was qualified according to her standards to pray for her. I ended up not praying for her. Being a believer and a minister was not enough for her. I also was not a pastor of a church. I started to question myself about what had happened. Then I concluded that I did what God told me. All we can do is obey what God tells us. She reacted like Naaman. If Naaman had chosen not to bathe in the Jordan, it would have been Naaman's fault that he didn't get healed. The account of Naaman shows us how what we expect affects our choices and what we will receive from God. But that expectation should be based on faith in God, not our pride or fears.

David, Bathsheba, and Uriah

The account in the Old Testament of David, Bathsheba, and Uriah shows the domino effect your choices can have. Most people have lined up dominos or seen them lined up in a straight line front to back, with the distance between each domino being about half their height. If you set up one hundred of them, the first domino can knock down the next domino, and that domino will knock down the next until the last domino has fallen. This account shows how one choice leads to another choice until you don't know how you got to where you are. We read about this account in 2 Samuel 11:1–17.

> It happened in the spring of the year, at
> the time when kings go out *to battle,* that David
> sent Joab and his servants with him, and all
> Israel; and they destroyed the people of Ammon

and besieged Rabbah. But David remained at Jerusalem. (2 Samuel 11:1)

Here in verse 1, David makes what seems to be an innocent choice to stay home from the battle. But this choice puts David where he wasn't supposed to be. The verse says it was the time of year that the kings would go out to battle. David should have been on the battlefield with his army. The following four verses give an account of the consequence of not going to war with his men.

> v. 2 Then it happened one evening that David arose from his bed and walked on the roof of the king's house. And from the roof he saw a woman bathing, and the woman *was* very beautiful to behold.
> v. 3 So David sent and inquired about the woman. And *someone* said, "*Is* this not Bathsheba, the daughter of Eliam, the wife of Uriah the Hittite?"
> v. 4 Then David sent messengers, and took her; and she came to him, and he lay with her, for she was cleansed from her impurity; and she returned to her house.
> v. 5 And the woman conceived; so she sent and told David, and said, "I *am* with child." (2 Samuel 11:2–5)

In verse 2, David gets bored and chooses to take a walk on the rooftop of his house. While taking his walk, he sees a beautiful woman bathing. In verses 3 and 4, David chooses to do something he shouldn't. He finds out who she is and invites her over to his house. He decided to invite Bathsheba over, knowing that she was married and to whom she was married. In verse 5, a domino falls that David didn't want to fall. Bathsheba gets pregnant. Next, David decides (chooses) to cover up his sin in 2 Samuel 11:6–13.

v. 6 Then David sent to Joab, *saying,* "Send me Uriah the Hittite." And Joab sent Uriah to David.

v. 7 When Uriah had come to him, David asked how Joab was doing, and how the people were doing, and how the war prospered.

v. 8 And David said to Uriah, "Go down to your house and wash your feet." So Uriah departed from the king's house, and a gift *of food* from the king followed him.

v. 9 But Uriah slept at the door of the king's house with all the servants of his lord, and did not go down to his house.

v. 10 So when they told David, saying, "Uriah did not go down to his house," David said to Uriah, "Did you not come from a journey? Why did you not go down to your house?" v. 11 And Uriah said to David, "The ark and Israel and Judah are dwelling in tents, and my lord Joab and the servants of my lord are encamped in the open fields. Shall I then go to my house to eat and drink, and to lie with my wife? *As* you live, and *as* your soul lives, I will not do this thing."

v. 12 Then David said to Uriah, "Wait here today also, and tomorrow I will let you depart." So Uriah remained in Jerusalem that day and the next.

v. 13 Now when David called him, he ate and drank before him; and he made him drunk. And at evening he went out to lie on his bed with the servants of his lord, but he did not go down to his house. (2 Samuel 6–13)

David's plan to cover up his bad choices was to have Uriah, Bathsheba's husband, return from the war so Uriah would sleep with his wife. Unfortunately for David, Uriah chooses to be more loyal to the other soldiers than David. Uriah wouldn't go home and sleep with his wife even after David got him drunk. In 2 Samuel 11:14–17, we discover how David chooses to resolve his problem.

> v. 14 In the morning it happened that David wrote a letter to Joab and sent *it* by the hand of Uriah.
> v. 15 And he wrote in the letter, saying, "Set Uriah in the forefront of the hottest battle, and retreat from him, that he may be struck down and die."
> v. 16 So it was, while Joab besieged the city, that he assigned Uriah to a place where he knew there *were* valiant men.
> v. 17 Then the men of the city came out and fought with Joab. And *some* of the people of the servants of David fell; and Uriah the Hittite died also. (2 Samuel 11:14–17)

David's choice for resolving the problem was to have Uriah killed in battle. He even had Uriah carry his death sentence to Joab, the battle commander. This situation would have never happened if David had done what he was supposed to do: go to battle like the other kings. David's desire for Bathsheba is an example of James 1:13–15.

> v. 13 Let no one say when he is tempted, "I am tempted by God"; for God cannot be tempted by evil, nor does He Himself tempt anyone.
> v. 14 But each one is tempted when he is drawn away by his own desires and enticed. v. 15 Then, when desire has conceived, it gives birth to sin; and sin, when it is full-grown, brings forth death. (James 1:13–15)

David's desire tempted him. David's desire that led to this series of sins was not his walking on the rooftop at night. David's desire that started this series of sins was his choice to give in to his flesh and stay in the comforts of home and not go to the battlefield as he should have. That choice led to choosing another desire and choosing another desire, followed by the death of Uriah. And later, the death of the baby.

You can see how making a bad choice can lead to more bad choices. When you find yourself in a situation that you shouldn't, think about David on the rooftop when he should have been with his army. Don't say, "I shouldn't have been on that rooftop." Determine what you should be doing. By doing what you should, you can avoid many negative consequences.

Imagine you're on your way to a restaurant. You are following the GPS directions, and the thought of a shortcut enters your mind. You decide to take what you think is a shortcut. You get lost and find yourself in a less-than-desirable area. You're driving along, and you get a flat. You open the trunk of your car, and you remember that you didn't repair your last flat. You close the trunk and notice some guys around the car. The next thing you know, you are being mugged. Now you are beaten and without any money. Your thought is *If only I didn't have a flat, I would not be in this situation.* Was it the flat that put you in that situation? You would have avoided the situation if you had remained on the GPS's path. Jesus told us that in this life, there would be tribulation. Since there will be tribulation, don't bring problems upon yourself. If there is going to be tribulation, let it be while following God's path.

I just discussed a handful of the many choices made in the Old Testament. Here are some of my other favorite accounts involving impressive choices. There is Rahab choosing to hide the two spies of Israel. She became the wife of one of the spies and part of the lineage of Jesus. Another favorite of mine is Abraham choosing to believe in God to the extent that he was willing to sacrifice his son. I am incredibly impressed by the choices made by the three Hebrew boys not to bow to the gold image of King Nebuchadnezzar, knowing that they would be thrown into a fiery furnace. I can't forget Daniel, who knew he would be thrown into the lion's den when people saw him. Yet he defied King Darius's decree of not praying to any god or human for thirty days and chose to continue his daily prayer habit. Our thoughts should be so ingrained with faith in God that we would stand for God at all costs.

CHAPTER 4

New Testament Choices

This chapter will discuss a few of the numerous choices people made in the New Testament. As you read about these people and their choices, consider the situation and put yourself in their place. Be honest and ask yourself, what would you choose in that situation?

Peter Walks on Water

With two loaves of bread and five fish, Jesus feeds five thousand men, plus women and children. Following the feeding of five thousand plus, we find in Matthew 14:22–31 the account of Jesus sending His disciples to the other side of the sea.

> v. 22 Immediately Jesus made His disciples get into the boat and go before Him to the other side, while He sent the multitudes away.
>
> v. 23 And when He had sent the multitudes away, He went up on the mountain by Himself to pray. Now when evening came, He was alone there.
>
> v. 24 But the boat was now in the middle of the sea, tossed by the waves, for the wind was contrary. (Matthew 14:22–24)

These three verses set the context for what is about to happen. In verse 22, we find that Jesus had to make the disciples get into the boat and go to the other side. Remember, some of the disciples were fishermen. These guys knew how to read the weather, and they knew a storm was coming and that the sea would not be safe. Yet the disciples chose to obey Jesus and set sail to the other side of the sea due to Jesus's persuading. Verse 24 informs us that a raging storm did manifest and that the boat was being tossed around by the waves. I am sure the disciples were doing all they knew to stay alive. Just as I am sure that the thought came to them that they had told Jesus that a storm was coming. We need to choose to trust in Jesus when natural things appear contrary to what the Word has said. Verses 25 through 28 tell us what happened before Peter walked on water.

> v. 25 Now in the fourth watch of the night Jesus went to them, walking on the sea.
>
> v. 26 And when the disciples saw Him walking on the sea, they were troubled, saying, "It is a ghost!" And they cried out for fear.
>
> v. 27 But immediately Jesus spoke to them, saying, "Be of good cheer! It is I; do not be afraid."
>
> v. 28 And Peter answered Him and said, "Lord, if it is You, command me to come to You on the water." (Matthew 14:25–28)

In verse 25, between 3:00 a.m. and 6:00 a.m., Jesus, going to the other side, walked on the sea. Verse 26 tells us that the disciples were afraid and cried out in fear when they saw Jesus walking on the sea. Because they thought they saw a ghost. Consider the disciples' situation. They are in the midst of a raging storm, thinking that they will die, when they see a figure in the shape of a man walking on water. I can understand their fear. When I was a kid, I remember waking up in the middle of the night and seeing a woman standing in my bedroom next to a chair. Then I noticed that her feet and the chair were not touching the floor. Seeing that, I started screaming. Only later to find out that it was a reflection from the moonlight of a picture of my great-grandmother. I still remember that, and that happened more than sixty years ago. I found fear in my heart, just like the disciples, when confronted with something totally out of the ordinary.

In verse 27, we find the disciples in fear and panic, so Jesus tells them, "Be of good cheer! It is I; do not be afraid." Jesus tells them to calm down because it was Him, and everything will be okay. What has always intrigued me is Peter's statement in verse 28. Peter chose to ask Jesus, "Lord, if it is you, command me to come to you on the water." Most people, or should I say if I were in that life-or-death situation, I think I would have said, "Jesus, save us." I believe that Peter's request must have come from a revelation that he could do whatever Jesus said he could do. That is the revelation that we should have. As believers, we need the revelation that, because Jesus is living in us, we can do whatever the Word of God says we can do and that we have what the Word of God says we have. We find Jesus's response in Matthew 14:29.

> So He said, "Come." And when Peter had
> come down out of the boat, he walked on the
> water to go to Jesus. (Matthew 14:29)

Jesus said, "Come." When you consider Peter's statement to Jesus, what else could Jesus say in response? Peter got out of the boat and walked toward Jesus. James chapter 2 tells us that faith without corresponding action is dead. In this case, Peter's faith in the word *come*, spoken by Jesus, would be dead without Peter choosing the corresponding action of getting out of the boat and walking on water. The following two verses show us what not to do when choosing to follow God's Word.

> v. 30 But when he saw that the wind *was*
> boisterous, he was afraid; and beginning to sink
> he cried out, saying, "Lord, save me!"
> v. 31 And immediately Jesus stretched out
> *His* hand and caught him, and said to him, "O

you of little faith, why did you doubt?" (Matthew
14:30–31)

Verse 30 informs us that at some point, while Peter was walking on water to Jesus, he began to see "the wind was boisterous" and chose to let fear enter into his thoughts. Peter was afraid because he took his eyes off Jesus and looked at the circumstances. I don't know about you, but I have never seen the wind boisterous. I have heard the wind, and I have seen the wind blow things around. My point is that we don't see the wind. We can feel the wind, hear the wind, and see what the wind is doing or has done. The verse also tells us that Peter began to sink. I have never seen anyone begin to sink. But the fact that scripture says that he began to sink implies that it was a process. There is a process of getting your eyes off Jesus and the spiritual world to having your eyes only on this natural world. Here is where Peter asks Jesus to save him.

In verse 31, Jesus reaches out, catches Peter, and says, "O you of little faith, why did you doubt?" So what is it that you must not do after you choose to follow God's Word? You must not doubt. Jesus asked Peter why he doubted. Peter doubted because he looked at the circumstances around him and became afraid. Fear comes from doubting God's Word. Second Timothy 1:7 tells us that God has not given us a spirit of fear. Fear is not of God. You must choose to reject fear and believe in God. You keep from doubting by choosing to focus on the word you received from God—in this case, that word was *come*—and to focus on the promises of God. Peter chose to move to the word *come*. But during his water walking experience, he let himself get distracted by waves and the sound caused by the strong blowing wind. When I say he allowed himself, I mean he chose to redirect his focus. Distractions often enter from our five natural senses and our thoughts. We must choose to do what 2 Corinthians 10:5 says to avoid distractions.

Casting down arguments and every high
thing that exalts itself against the knowledge of

God, bringing every thought into captivity to the obedience of Christ. (2 Corinthians 10:5)

Yes, we must choose to take those distractive and negative thoughts captive and eject them from our minds. Thoughts will come to your mind that contradict God's plan. When negative thoughts come, you have to choose to (1) reject those negative thoughts, (2) focus on the plan God has given you, and (3) trust that God will help you accomplish the plan. You have to follow the plan. You will also always have to keep your eyes on Jesus. Jesus is our example and our standard. We can accomplish whatever Jesus, the Word of God made flesh, says we can accomplish. What Jesus says we have, we have, and we are who He says we are. Choose to keep your eyes on Jesus and walk on water. Your water is whatever arises to prevent you from accomplishing what the Holy Spirit has planned for you.

Saul's Conversion

Now I will discuss the conversion of Saul in the book of Acts. But first, to get perspective on the situation, you need to know about Saul of Tarsus. We have Paul's, previously known as Saul, own words to tell us about himself. Let's see what Paul says in Acts 22:3–5.

> v. 3 I am indeed a Jew, born in Tarsus of Cilicia, but brought up in this city at the feet of Gamaliel, taught according to the strictness of our fathers' law, and was zealous toward God as you all are today.
> v. 4 I persecuted this Way to the death, binding and delivering into prisons both men and women,
> v. 5 as also the high priest bears me witness, and all the council of the elders, from whom I also received letters to the brethren, and went to

> Damascus to bring in chains even those who were
> there to Jerusalem to be punished. (Acts 22:3–5)

Paul, in these three verses, describes to us his lineage. He tells us that he is a Jew by birth and that Gamaliel taught him from a young child. Gamaliel, at that time, was the most notable teacher of the Mosaic law. The verse says that he was "taught according to the strictness of our father's law." This section of verse 3 in the King James Bible reads, "taught according to the perfect manner of the law of the fathers." Note that *fathers'* (NKJV) and *fathers* (KJV) both start with a lowercase *f*. If they had started with a capital *F*, they would be referring to Father God. But here they are talking about human fathers. Thus, Saul was taught all of the ceremonies and traditions of the law. Paul also tells us that he was a zealot, which means that he vehemently held to the standards he was taught. Saul's being a zealot is why he persecuted those of the Way to the fullest extent that he could. Those of the Way were those that chose to believe that Jesus was the Christ and attempted to live the lifestyle Jesus demonstrated. Saul had people put to death and imprisoned without regard to sex. Paul told the people that if they didn't believe that he had done these things, his witnesses were the high priests and the elders.

In Philippians 3:4–6, Saul, then known as Paul, says,

> v. 4 Though I also might have confidence in the flesh. If anyone else thinks he may have confidence in the flesh, I more so:
> v. 5 circumcised the eighth day, of the stock of Israel, *of* the tribe of Benjamin, a Hebrew of the Hebrews; concerning the law, a Pharisee;
> v. 6 concerning zeal, persecuting the church; concerning the righteousness which is in the law, blameless. (Philippians 3:4–6)

Again in these verses, Paul talks about his heritage. Paul is telling us that he was circumcised on the eighth day according to the law. And that he was born "of the stock of Israel," meaning that no non-Hebrew was in his heritage. Paul also tells us that he is from the tribe of Benjamin. There are many things that Paul could have meant by saying he was from the stock of Israel, such as being from a tribe that came from Jacobs's wife Rachel, but it also speaks to his pride in his heritage. Paul tells us that not only was he a Hebrew, but he upheld the Hebrew language and customs. He also tells us he was a Pharisee, the strictest sect of his religion. In verse 6 again, Paul talks about his ruthless and unwavering persecution of the church. He tells the believers of Philippi this because he wanted them to know that if anyone could have confidence in their salvation through the flesh, it would be him.

This segment of scripture shows us how strongly Saul identified with his heritage in the flesh and his lifelong training. I reviewed these passages because I wanted you to understand Paul—who he was, his background and what he rejected to follow Jesus. With this understanding, you can have a greater appreciation for what happened to Paul, then called Saul, on his way to Damascus in Acts 9:1–8.

> v. 1 Then Saul, still breathing threats and murder against the disciples of the Lord, went to the high priest
>
> v. 2 and asked letters from him to the synagogues of Damascus, so that if he found any who were of the Way, whether men or women, he might bring them bound to Jerusalem.
>
> v. 3 As he journeyed he came near Damascus, and suddenly a light shone around him from heaven.
>
> v. 4 Then he fell to the ground, and heard a voice saying to him, "Saul, Saul, why are you persecuting Me?"
>
> v. 5 And he said, "Who are You, Lord?" Then the Lord said, "I am Jesus, whom you are persecuting. It *is* hard for you to kick against the goads."

> v. 6 So he, trembling and astonished, said, "Lord, what do You want me to do?" Then the Lord *said* to him, "Arise and go into the city, and you will be told what you must do."
>
> v. 7 And the men who journeyed with him stood speechless, hearing a voice but seeing no one.
>
> v. 8 Then Saul arose from the ground, and when his eyes were opened he saw no one. But they led him by the hand and brought *him* into Damascus. (Acts 9:1–8)

I like Saul's choice of responses during his encounter with Jesus on the road to Damascus. In verse 4, he chooses to humble himself and falls to the ground. I imagine him either prostrate, facedown on the ground, or on his knees, bowed facedown, in response to the great light from heaven surrounding him. Saul could have been proud and defiant by standing firm and demanding to know what was happening. He could have chosen that defiant posture and attitude you choose when someone gives you sound advice that is not what you wanted to hear. Then in verse 5, Saul, still humbling himself, responds to Jesus's question of "Saul, Saul, why are you persecuting Me?" by asking "Who are You, Lord?" You can see that Saul continued in his humble attitude. We should take our example from Saul and humble ourselves before the Lord.

In response to Saul's question, Jesus tells Saul, "I am Jesus, whom you are persecuting. It *is* hard for you to kick against the goads." Then Saul asks, "Lord, what do You want me to do?" That is a question we all should ask of God. I like Saul's response because he didn't attempt to defend his actions. He didn't say I was being a good Jew, cleansing the world of those who were not walking strictly to the law. Instead, Saul gave an attitude of repentance and asked what he should do. When told what he was to do, he didn't discuss other options but chose to obey. Because he was now blind, the men with him led him by the hand to Damascus. I love Saul's choosing to repent and obey the Lord. Here is a man who had every advantage and opportunity to be at the height of worldly success as far as the world could tell. But when he encountered Jesus, he gave it all up to join those he had been persecuting. I can almost hear you thinking, *If I had that type of encounter with God, I would choose to change to the extent that Saul did.* Any encounter with Jesus is enough to change you to the extent that Saul changed. If you compare your experience with Saul's experience, you are thinking naturally, not spiritually. Today we have the written Word of God. It is the power of the Word of God that changes a man.

Look at Luke 16, where Jesus gives the parable of the rich man and Lazarus. The parable is about a rich man and a poor man named Lazarus. They both die. The rich man goes to Hades and is tormented in flames while Lazarus is in the comfort of Abraham's bosom. The rich man requests the Lord to have Lazarus bring him a taste of water, but Lazarus cannot. Let's read Luke 16:27–30.

> v. 27 Then he [the rich man] said, "I beg you therefore, father, that you would send him [Lazarus] to my father's house,
>
> v. 28 for I have five brothers, that he may testify to them, lest they also come to this place of torment."
>
> v. 29 Abraham said to him, "They have Moses and the prophets; let them hear them."
>
> v. 30 And he said, "No, father Abraham; but if one goes to them from the dead, they will repent."
>
> v. 31 But he said to him, "If they do not hear Moses and the prophets, neither will they be persuaded though one rise from the dead." (Luke 16:27–31, parentheses are mine)

In verses 27 and 28, the rich man attempts to have Abraham send Lazarus to his family so that the rich man's brothers would not follow him to Hades. Abraham informs the rich man that his brothers only have to listen to what Moses and the prophets have said. We just have to hear what the Bible, God's Word, and the Holy Spirit say. The rich man believes that if someone from the dead were to go and confront his brothers, they would repent. We might think that if a person had the type of encounter with Jesus that Paul had, they would undoubtedly repent. But verse 31 tells us that if a person doesn't hear from the Bible or the Holy Spirit, that person will not choose to repent. A Saul-like experience with Jesus will not cause them to choose to repent. Saul repented because his heart's desire was always to do whatever God would have him do.

Ananias Goes to Saul

After discussing Saul, this is an excellent time to discuss Ananias. To me, Ananias represents the everyday believer that is a disciple of Jesus. Ananias shows that any disciple of Jesus may be called on to perform extraordinary tasks. You don't have to have a megachurch, have a television ministry, be a traveling minister, a doctor, or a professional athlete to work for Jesus. God uses people from all careers and all stations in life to do His work here on the earth. Acts 9:10–18 discusses the choice Ananias made.

> v. 10 Now there was a certain disciple at Damascus named Ananias; and to him the Lord said in a vision, "Ananias." And he said, "Here I am, Lord."
>
> v. 11 So the Lord *said* to him, "Arise and go to the street called Straight, and inquire at the house of Judas for *one* called Saul of Tarsus, for behold, he is praying.
>
> v. 12 And in a vision he has seen a man named Ananias coming in and putting *his* hand on him, so that he might receive his sight."
>
> v. 13 Then Ananias answered, "Lord, I have heard from many about this man, how much harm he has done to Your saints in Jerusalem.

v. 14 And here he has authority from the chief priests to bind all who call on Your name."

v. 15 But the Lord said to him, "Go, for he is a chosen vessel of Mine to bear My name before Gentiles, kings, and the children of Israel.

v. 16 For I will show him how many things he must suffer for My name's sake."

v. 17 And Ananias went his way and entered the house; and laying his hands on him he said, "Brother Saul, the Lord Jesus, who appeared to you on the road as you came, has sent me that you may receive your sight and be filled with the Holy Spirit."

v. 18 Immediately there fell from his eyes *something* like scales, and he received his sight at once; and he arose and was baptized. (Acts 9:10–18)

Verse 10 starts with "There was a certain disciple at Damascus named Ananias." The verse tells us that he was just a disciple. No title or status in the community of Jesus's followers is mentioned. Acts 22:12 tells us that Ananias was devout and had a good testimony. Jesus calls on His disciples not based on status or hierarchy but based on their relationship with Him. Because Ananias had a good relationship with the Lord, he recognized the Lord's voice when He called.

In verses 11 and 12, Jesus instructs Ananias where he would find Saul of Tarsus. Also, the verse informs us that Saul would be expecting him, and he is to lay hands on Saul so that Saul would regain sight. Have you ever been told to go and lay hands on someone and pray for them? I have. I would love to say that each time I heard God say to pray for someone, I did. But I haven't. I remember one time I was out shopping, and God wanted me to go pray for a lady. I managed to talk my way out of doing that. What I did was to choose not to obey the leading of the Holy Spirit. There is always some risk in obedience. In a store, there is the thought of the embarrassment of it not working or the person saying no.

Ananias's risk was much more significant. Earlier in the chapter, I talked about how Saul ruthlessly persecuted the believers. The fact is that Saul was out to do great harm to the followers of Jesus. In verse 13, Ananias chose a careful response to the command of Jesus. Ananias asks the Lord if He had heard what Saul has been doing to the saints in Jerusalem. Being that the Lord knows the heart of all men makes this an interesting question. Ananias knew from the experience of others that this would be putting his life into the hands of Saul. Jesus told Ananias to get up and go. Ananias chose to obey and went to Saul. Looking back on the situation, you could say that Ananias had the privilege of praying for Saul, who became Paul and wrote most of the New Testament.

Choosing Barabbas over Jesus

The account of Jesus's last Passover celebration and the time of His crucifixion is fascinating. There are so many things that happened during that time. A couple of things that happened show how moody crowds are. One day Jesus was being celebrated by a crowd choosing to sing to Him, "Hosanna! Blessed is He who comes in the name of the Lord." A few days later, a crowd with, most likely, some of those same people chose to have Barabbas pardoned instead of Jesus and then cried out to have Jesus crucified. We will start reading about this account in Matthew 21:1–13, five days before Passover.

> v. 1 Now when they drew near Jerusalem, and came to Bethphage, at the Mount of Olives, then Jesus sent two disciples,
>
> v. 2 saying to them, "Go into the village opposite you, and immediately you will find a donkey tied, and a colt with her. Loose *them* and bring *them* to Me.

v. 3 And if anyone says anything to you, you shall say, 'The Lord has need of them,' and immediately he will send them."

v. 4 All this was done that it might be fulfilled which was spoken by the prophet, saying:

v. 5 "TELL THE DAUGHTER OF ZION, 'BEHOLD, YOUR KING IS COMING TO YOU, LOWLY, AND SITTING ON A DONKEY, A COLT, THE FOAL OF A DONKEY.'"

v. 6 So the disciples went and did as Jesus commanded them.

v. 7 They brought the donkey and the colt, laid their clothes on them, and set *Him* on them.

v. 8 And a very great multitude spread their clothes on the road; others cut down branches from the trees and spread *them* on the road.

v. 9 Then the multitudes who went before and those who followed cried out, saying: "Hosanna to the Son of David! 'BLESSED IS HE WHO COMES IN THE NAME OF THE LORD!' Hosanna in the highest!"

v. 10 And when He had come into Jerusalem, all the city was moved, saying, "Who is this?"

v. 11 So the multitudes said, "This is Jesus, the prophet from Nazareth of Galilee."

v. 12 Then Jesus went into the temple of God and drove out all those who bought and sold in the temple, and overturned the tables of the money changers and the seats of those who sold doves.

13 And He said to them, "It is written, 'MY HOUSE SHALL BE CALLED A HOUSE OF PRAYER,' but you have made it a 'DEN OF THIEVES.'" (Matthew 21:1–13)

Here we find Jesus continuing to follow the will of the Father. Jesus knows that this is His last Passover celebration. Verses 8 and 9 inform us that a great multitude had gathered to cheer on Jesus as He came to Jerusalem. The crowd was throwing down their clothes, cutting off branches, and throwing them onto the road in front of Jesus as He rode on the donkey into Jerusalem and as the crowd cheered and sang a song to Him. They were cheering because of the wonderful works He had done. Verse 11 tells us that the people viewed Jesus as a prophet. This celebration of Jesus entering Jerusalem was humanity celebrating Jesus for what they expected Him to accomplish. Today we celebrate the Lamb sacrificed for the salvation of the world. We celebrate Jesus for what He came to do and did accomplish.

Now the Pharisees choose to be angry with Jesus. What He did in verses 12 and 13 got them enraged. Jesus went to the temple and violently threw out those buying and selling. Then He exclaimed that His house was to be called a house of prayer and that they had turned it into a den of thieves. By calling the temple His house, He was saying that He was God because the temple was the house of God.

The chief priest and elders manage to have Jesus arrested and taken to Pontius Pilate, the governor. Pilate knew that the Jews had turned Jesus over to him because of jealousy, as we will read in Matthew 27:15–26.

v. 15 Now at the feast the governor was accustomed to releasing to the multitude one prisoner whom they wished.

v. 16 And at that time they had a notorious prisoner called Barabbas.

v. 17 Therefore, when they had gathered together, Pilate said to them, "Whom do you want me to release to you? Barabbas, or Jesus who is called Christ?"

v. 18 For he knew that they had handed Him over because of envy.

v. 19 While he was sitting on the judgment seat, his wife sent to him, saying, "Have nothing to do with that just Man, for I have suffered many things today in a dream because of Him."

v. 20 But the chief priests and elders persuaded the multitudes that they should ask for Barabbas and destroy Jesus.

v. 21 The governor answered and said to them, "Which of the two do you want me to release to you?" They said, "Barabbas!"

v. 22 Pilate said to them, "What then shall I do with Jesus who is called Christ?" *They* all said to him, "Let Him be crucified!"

v. 23 Then the governor said, "Why, what evil has He done?" But they cried out all the more, saying, "Let Him be crucified!"

v. 24 When Pilate saw that he could not prevail at all, but rather *that* a tumult was rising, he took water and washed *his* hands before the multitude, saying, "I am innocent of the blood of this just Person. You see *to it*."

v. 25 And all the people answered and said, "His blood *be* on us and on our children."

v. 26 Then he released Barabbas to them; and when he had scourged Jesus, he delivered *Him* to be crucified. (Matthew 27:15–26)

In verses 15 to 18, Pilate attempted to diplomatically release Jesus and stay on the good side of the Jewish leaders. Pilate as governor was accustomed to releasing a prisoner at that time of year. Knowing that Jesus had done nothing wrong, Pilate thought that if he gave the people the choice of releasing Jesus, a good man, or Barabbas, a notorious criminal, surely they would choose to have Jesus released. In verse 17, Pilate gave the crowd the choice of releasing Jesus or Barabbas. But in verse 21, the crowd, being persuaded by the chief priests and elders, chose to have Barabbas released. Instead of doing what he knew was right, Pilate chose not to cross the Jewish leaders. When Pilate, in verse 22, asked the people what he should do with Jesus, they said to crucify Him. In the next verse, with a louder volume, they said to crucify Jesus. The crowd, persuaded by the chief priest and elders against Jesus, chose to have the blood of Jesus on their own hands.

How would you like to have a few days as Jesus had? One day you are having a ticker-tape parade down Fifth Avenue in New York City for winning the baseball World Series. But a few influential people don't like all the praise you are getting. So they start a rumor and put out some false evidence against you. Three days later, you are in court, and there is a massive crowd outside the courthouse screaming for you to be in prison. That's a tremendous turn of events. In Jesus's situation, the crowd chose to celebrate Him one day, and then without warning, the crowd decided to have Him put to death. Jesus chose to follow the will of the Father no matter what the consequences. We must determine in our hearts to do the same.

The Women with the Issue of Blood

I will now discuss the woman who, after many failed attempts to get healed, decided that Jesus was her answer. Place yourself in her situation: You have a plague, and the law states that you can't go out in public, and if you do, you must yell "unclean, unclean" when you are close to people, or you can be put to death. You are told there is a mega rally at the stadium downtown, and the speaker has healed many people. What would you choose to do? In Mark chapter 5, a woman is facing a similar situation. The setting starts at the shore. Jesus has just crossed the sea, and when He gets off the boat, a vast crowd surrounds Him. Jairus, one of the synagogue rulers, comes to Jesus, falls at His feet, and begs Jesus to go home with him to heal his daughter, who is close to death. The crowd walking with Jesus on His way to Jairus's house is massive and packed together. We read in Mark 5:24–34 what happened.

v. 24 So *Jesus* went with him, and a great multitude followed Him and thronged Him.

v. 25 Now a certain woman had a flow of blood for twelve years,

v. 26 and had suffered many things from many physicians. She had spent all that she had and was no better, but rather grew worse.

v. 27 When she heard about Jesus, she came behind *Him* in the crowd and touched His garment.

v. 28 For she said, "If only I may touch His clothes, I shall be made well."

v. 29 Immediately the fountain of her blood was dried up, and she felt in *her* body that she was healed of the affliction.

v. 30 And Jesus, immediately knowing in Himself that power had gone out of Him, turned around in the crowd and said, "Who touched My clothes?"

v. 31 But His disciples said to Him, "You see the multitude thronging You, and You say, 'Who touched Me?'"

v. 32 And He looked around to see her who had done this thing.

v. 33 But the woman, fearing and trembling, knowing what had happened to her, came and fell down before Him and told Him the whole truth.

v. 34 And He said to her, "Daughter, your faith has made you well. Go in peace, and be healed of your affliction." (Mark 5:24–34)

Verses 24 to 26 tell us that the crowd was a multitude and that they were thronging Jesus. That means that the crowd was huge, squeezed together tightly, and touching Jesus on all sides. The verse also tells us that her illness was a flow of blood and that she had the illness for twelve years. From these verses, I tend to think that, at first, she was well-off financially, and she had an unshakeable desire for healing. Because of her desire to be healed, she chose to go through many kinds of treatments. She also spent all her money on those treatments. However, her illness only got worse. Verses 27 and 28 tell us that she had learned of another way to get healed. People told her that Jesus could heal her. She most likely had been told by people healed by Jesus or people who had seen people healed by Jesus. She specifically was told that she would be healed if she touched Jesus's garment. The most important thing was that she chose to believe what she had heard about Jesus. We know this from her two actions. First, she chose to speak what she believed by saying, "If only I may touch His clothes, I shall be made well." I think that she said this multiple times to herself as she was going to where she would attempt to touch Jesus. Second, she chose to act on what she believed by doing what she said. James chapter 2 tells us that faith without corresponding action is dead. Her touching the bottom of Jesus's robe was her corresponding action. She knew that attempting this action could cause her death. Luke 8:44 says that she touched the border of His garment. We would refer to the border of a garment as the fringe or edge of His robe. Which leads many to believe that she was on her hands and knees, forcing her way through the crowd.

Continuing in the story, we are told in verses 29 through 34 what took place after she touched the fringe of Jesus's robe. Immediately, the flow of blood stopped, and she could feel healing in her body. Also, immediately Jesus noticed that power had been drawn out of Him, and He asked, "Who touched My clothes?" The disciples were amazed that Jesus would ask such a question because so many people were touching Him. Knowing what happened to her, the woman confessed that she had touched Jesus and testified about what she had done. Then Jesus told her why she received healing. He said, "Daughter, your faith has made you well. Go in peace and be healed of your affliction." She had chosen faith and the corresponding action to what she believed. Notice that Jesus didn't say that He had healed her. He said that her faith had healed her.

You might ask yourself why more of the people touching Jesus didn't get healed. The other people didn't believe in their hearts that they would be healed by touching Jesus or His clothes. They might have had head knowledge but did not believe in their heart that touching Jesus would heal them. There is a difference between knowing and believing. Knowledge is intellectual and is in your head. Believing is in the heart and can be heard in what you say and seen in your actions. The women with the issue of blood chose to say, "If only I may touch His clothes, I shall be made well." Note that her statement there was not a maybe. She didn't say, "Well, if this doesn't work, I will try something else." Today, many people choose to google their illness, which focuses on the problem and not on Jesus, who is the solution to the problem. She could have been like Peter and had chosen to take her focus off Jesus and had her focus on the massive crowd and how squeezed together the crowd was. Which most likely would have led to a decision to give up. The second thing she chose was to force her way through the crowd and touch Jesus's robe. She didn't get close to Jesus and choose to stop and think, *I am close enough, why aren't I healed?* She forced her way to Jesus. Make up your mind to be as determined as this woman for your healing.

I hope you have received revelation from these accounts into your choice-making process. Take time and study other accounts, such as Mary, who chose to believe the angel and became the mother of Jesus. I give a lot of honor to Joseph, who chose to believe the angel and took Mary as his wife and raised Jesus as his son. There are the 120 who choose to wait as Jesus had instructed and were baptized with the Holy Spirit. How about Paul and Silas, who choose to pray and praise God when thrown into prison. There is Judas, who made a bad choice and sold out Jesus. There are so many examples of choices people made in the New Testament, but the choices that matter most are your choices.

CHAPTER 5

You Get to Choose (Part 1)

Here you are, a star football player, about to graduate from high school. You have several scholarships from several universities from which to choose. You can only pick one. Your parents tell you that it is your choice and have informed you that your choice will affect the rest of your life. Which scholarship should you pick? Some universities are known for their academics, and some universities can take you to the next level in your sport. Some schools are known for having the best parties, and there are those in beautiful locations. Many variables will determine which university you will choose. It is a tough decision, but you must choose. The same applies to your life because God gave us the freedom of choice. In this and the next chapter of this book, I will discuss a few of the numerous choices indicated in the Bible that we have as humans.

To Serve the Lord

The number one and most significant choice you will make is to choose to serve the Lord. When we read the Bible, we read about people who have chosen to serve the Lord and those that have chosen not to serve the Lord. We all come into the world not serving the Lord. We all rebelled against God because we were in Adam when Adam rebelled against God in the garden. Many people are surprised when they learn that we were all born infected with sin. We didn't choose to be born into sin, but we were. The good news is we can be cured of our sin infection; we have that choice. In Joshua 24:14–15, Joshua asks the people of Israel if they will serve the god of this world through sin or the true God through obedience.

> v. 14 Now therefore, fear the LORD, serve Him in sincerity and in truth, and put away the gods which your fathers served on the other side of the River and in Egypt. Serve the LORD!
> v. 15 And if it seems evil to you to serve the LORD, choose for yourselves this day whom you will serve, whether the gods which your fathers served that *were* on the other side of the River, or the gods of the Amorites, in whose land you dwell. But as for me and my house, we will serve the LORD. (Joshua 24:14–15)

Joshua tells the people that they need to choose to reverence God and serve Him with all their hearts and stop serving the gods they left in Egypt. He tells the people this by asking them *whom will they serve*. That is a question we should ask ourselves. We have to choose every day and sometimes multiple times a day whom we will serve.

When we are born-again, we have chosen Jesus as our Lord and Savior, and God gives us the grace needed to live out His desires for us. Our old spirit man passed away and was made new when we were born-again. Being born-again, we have to reprogram our soul (our mind, will, and emotions) and buffet (take control of) our bodies.

Many of us have lived a life serving our flesh and engaging in behavior that pleases the devil. Our mind must be renewed from the programming of this world. However, the response we choose should be the same as Joshua's response: "As for me and my house, we will serve the LORD." In the following few verses of Joshua 24, the people of Israel rehearsed the mighty works that God had done for them. If you are born-again, you should review your life for the things God has done in your life. The best thing God did for all of us is to give

His only Son so that those who choose to believe in Him will have eternal life.

God allows us to choose between His ways and our natural or worldly ways, which the devil influences through deception. Our natural and worldly ways are not God's ways. In Isaiah 55:9, God tells us that His ways are higher than our ways and that His thoughts are higher than our thoughts. Yet in 1 Corinthians 2:16, we are told that those that are born-again have the mind of Christ. This might appear to be a contradiction, but it shows the contrast between our natural mind and our born-again spirit. God's ways are higher than our natural mind, but we have His mind in our born-again spirit. We must choose to do what Romans 12:2 says.

> And do not be conformed to this world, but
> be transformed by the renewing of your mind,
> that you may prove what *is* that good and accept-
> able and perfect will of God. (Romans 12:2)

The verse tells us that our natural thoughts and action conform to this world, and we have to renew our natural mind so that it thinks like the mind of Christ, that is, the mind of our spirit man. To renew your mind, you will choose to read, study, and meditate on God's Word. You will have to read God's Word, listen to biblically-based messages, and do what the Holy Spirit reveals to you. God is not going to renew your mind automatically. You must choose to do whatever you must to have your mind renewed. God renewed your spirit. You have to renew your mind.

Saul is an excellent example of getting one's mind renewed. Remember our earlier discussion about Saul. Paul (Saul) was a Pharisee trained from his childhood by Gamaliel, the greatest teacher of Jewish law. Saul considered himself a Hebrew of Hebrews, which means that Saul ingrained himself in his heritage, the Jewish laws and the Jewish customs. Because of Gamaliel's teaching, Saul also had excellent knowledge of the Old Testament. Now that he was a believer in Jesus, his mind would need renewing to Jesus's teachings.

Galatians 1:15–18 gives us some insight into what Saul did to renew his mind.

> v. 15 But when it pleased God, who separated me from my mother's womb and called *me* through His grace,
> v. 16 to reveal His Son in me, that I might preach Him among the Gentiles, I did not immediately confer with flesh and blood,
> v. 17 nor did I go up to Jerusalem to those *who were* apostles before me; but I went to Arabia, and returned again to Damascus.
> v. 18 Then after three years I went up to Jerusalem to see Peter, and remained with him fifteen days. (Galatians 1:15–18)

These verses tell us that Saul didn't at first get his teaching from other men. He went to Arabia and later returned to Damascus. In those three years, Saul started using his Greek name, Paul. Paul received his teaching from the Holy Spirit, and subsequently, he conferred with the disciples. I am sure that after Saul's conversion, when he read the scriptures, the Holy Spirit revealed things that pointed to Jesus, Jesus's purpose for coming to the world and things about the kingdom of God.

Today God has given us apostles, prophets, evangelists, pastors, and teachers to help us receive revelation into the Word of God. The Holy Spirit that Saul, you, and I have received is our most essential teacher. But we need ministers because when we receive Jesus as Lord, most of us have not had the training in the scriptures that Saul (Paul) had received from Gamaliel. And like Paul, we must choose to hear and do what the Holy Spirit says.

The more we renew our minds, the greater our ability to serve the Lord according to His will. Remember that when Saul was persecuting the followers of Jesus, he thought he was following the will of God. But after he had an encounter with Jesus and renewed his mind, he chose to follow the will of the Lord Jesus. Saul became Paul and changed from working to destroy the followers of Jesus to doing all he could to serve Jesus.

To Seek the Kingdom of God

People generally tend to choose to worry about many things. We tend to worry about money, home, food, work, clothes, relationships, etc. Worrying doesn't change what you are worried about, but worrying can negatively affect you physically and mentally. Worrying also negatively affects those that are around you. In Matthew 6:25–33, God tells us there is something you should do before getting drawn into worry.

v. 25 Therefore I say to you, do not worry about your life, what you will eat or what you will drink; nor about your body, what you will put on. Is not life more than food and the body more than clothing?

v. 26 Look at the birds of the air, for they neither sow nor reap nor gather into barns; yet your heavenly Father feeds them. Are you not of more value than they?

v. 27 Which of you by worrying can add one cubit to his stature?

v. 28 So why do you worry about clothing? Consider the lilies of the field, how they grow: they neither toil nor spin;

v. 29 and yet I say to you that even Solomon in all his glory was not arrayed like one of these.

v. 30 Now if God so clothes the grass of the field, which today is, and tomorrow is thrown into the oven, *will He* not much more *clothe* you, O you of little faith?

> v. 31 Therefore do not worry, saying, "What
> shall we eat?" or "What shall we drink?" or "What
> shall we wear?"
>
> v. 32 For after all these things the Gentiles
> seek. For your heavenly Father knows that you
> need all these things.
>
> v. 33 But seek first the kingdom of God and
> His righteousness, and all these things shall be
> added to you. (Matthew 6:25–33)

In verse 25, God tells us not to worry about the natural things in life. Because life is more than the natural things in this world, God, in verses 26–30, describes the care He gives to the things in nature and how much more He cares for us. Then two verses down, God says that the unbelievers worry about natural things. As believers, we shouldn't worry about natural things because He knows what we need. In verse 33, God tells us "to seek first His kingdom and His righteousness," and the things we desire will be given to us. One amazing thing is what you desire can change. As you choose to seek the kingdom of God, God will change your desires. God will take your desires and replace them with His desire for you. Here is how I translate Matthew 6:33.

> But make the principal focus in your life
> striving after the kingdom of God, which is righ-
> teousness, peace, and joy in the Holy Ghost, and
> all the things you need will be given to you.

So the question is, why are we worried? God knows what we need, and when we choose to know and understand the kingdom of God and His righteousness, our worldly desires are replaced by godly desires. Matthew 6:33 says to seek first. What does that mean to you? Seeking is attempting to find or get something. So to seek is the active process of searching to find something. Matthew 7:7–8 tells us what will happen when we seek what we desire.

> v. 7 Ask, and it will be given to you; seek, and you will find; knock, and it will be opened to you.
>
> v. 8 For everyone who asks receives, and he who seeks finds, and to him who knocks it will be opened. (Matthew 7:7–8)

These two verses tell us that if we seek, we will find. But how are we to seek? Proverbs 2:3–5 says that if you want discernment and understanding, you have to seek them like seeking silver and hidden treasure.

> v. 3 Yes, if you cry out for discernment, *And* lift up your voice for understanding,
>
> v. 4 If you seek her as silver, And search for her as *for* hidden treasures;
>
> v. 5 Then you will understand the fear of the LORD, And find the knowledge of God. (Proverbs 2:3–5)

So we are to seek as if we are looking for hidden treasure. The things of the kingdom of God are not hidden from us but hidden for us. If we seek the kingdom of God as we would seek hidden treasure, we will find it. When we seek God's kingdom, we are searching for the most valuable thing a man can find. There was a time in the United States that men and women would sell everything they owned to go west, attempting to find gold. Today many people from a young age choose to train for hours every day to fine-tune their bodies and perfect their skills to become professional athletes, singers, or actors to gain fame and money. Others dedicate many years of postgraduate study to become things such as doctors and lawyers. This shows that when people desire to achieve a goal, people will choose to discipline themselves to whatever is needed to obtain that goal. The seeking of the knowledge of the Word of God and a close relationship with God is no different. Here is what Paul in 1 Corinthians 9:24 says. We will read these verses in the AMPC Bible.

> v. 24 Do you not know that in a race all the runners compete, but [*only*] one receives the prize? So run [*your race*] that you may lay hold [*of the prize*] *and* make it yours.
>
> v. 25 Now every athlete who goes into training
>
> conducts himself temperately *and* restricts himself in all things. They do it to win a wreath that will soon wither, but we [*do it to receive a crown of eternal blessedness*] that cannot wither.
>
> v. 26 Therefore I do not run uncertainly (without definite aim). I do not box like one beating the air *and* striking without an adversary.
>
> v. 27 But [*like a boxer*] I buffet my body [*handle it roughly, discipline it by hardships*] and subdue it, for fear that after proclaiming to others the Gospel *and* things pertaining to it, I myself should become unfit [*not stand the test, be unapproved and rejected as a counterfeit*]. (1 Corinthians 9:24–27 AMPC)

These are awesome verses. They tell us how we are to be seeking. We are to be seeking as if we're training to win first place in a race. Paul says "training to win in a race." Paul is telling us that when a person trains for a race, they train with the intent to win first prize. What does that look like to you? I ask the question because it looks different for everyone. It depends on what race God has planned for you. Years ago, my daughter was in gymnastics. She trained at the same gym where an Olympic gymnast trained. They were training in the same gym for the same events but with different routines. A new gymnast, like a new believer, has fundamentals that need to be learned to become an Olympic gymnast or a mature believer. In gymnastics, you start at level 1 and progress to level 10. When you become proficient at one level, you advance to the next level. As believers, we mature from faith to faith, and we should always be maturing. But in our choosing to seek the kingdom of God, we are not in competition with other people. Our prize is to have Jesus say to us, "Well done," as He said in Matthew 25:21 and 23.

> His lord said to him, "Well *done,* good and faithful servant; you were faithful over a few things, I will make you ruler over many things. Enter into the joy of your lord." (Matthew 25:21)

and

> His lord said to him, "Well *done,* good and faithful servant; you have been faithful over a few things, I will make you ruler over many things. Enter into the joy of your lord." (Matthew 25:23)

People often, I was once told, live in a nongrowth environment. That is to say they stop growing. People often, after they graduate from high school or college, stop learning. They stop reading and studying. Thus, they stop growing and maturing. They stop seeking to improve themselves. Hebrews 5:12–14 speaks about those who stop maturing.

> v. 12 For though by this time you ought to be teachers, you need *someone* to teach you again the first principles of the oracles of God; and you have come to need milk and not solid food.
>
> v. 13 For everyone who partakes *only* of milk *is* unskilled in the word of righteousness, for he is a babe.
>
> v. 14 But solid food belongs to those who are of full age, *that is,* those who by reason of use have their senses exercised to discern both good and evil. (Hebrews 5:12–14)

These scriptures indicate that new believers are too mature, from babes feeding on the milk of the Word to mature believers feeding on the solid food of the Word. As a new believer, you are to read and study the Bible, and you will receive revelation knowledge about what the scriptures are saying. As you continue reading and studying God's Word, you will receive more and more revelation knowledge, and you will mature in your understanding of what the scriptures mean.

I have discussed the word *seek* in Matthew 6:33. The next word in that scripture is *first*. The first time I read Matthew 6:33, I thought it was speaking about "first thing in the morning." *First* could refer to being first in time, place, order, or importance. The word *first* also indicates seeking the kingdom of God before seeking other things in life. *First* can be first place, first thing, or early in your life. Some of the best times to seek the kingdom of God and His righteousness is as early in your life as you can, before you start your day or before any decision and all day long. David, in Psalm 63:1, said he would seek God early.

> O God, You *are* my God; Early will I seek
> You; My soul thirsts for You; My flesh longs for
> You In a dry and thirsty land Where there is no
> water. (Psalm 63:1)

Jesus, our example, also sought God the Father early. There are times when Jesus got up early and prayed. There were also times when Jesus stayed up all night spending time in prayer with God the Father. These two scriptures are examples of these prayer times.

> Now in the morning, having risen a long
> while before daylight, He went out and departed to
> a solitary place; and there He prayed. (Mark 1:35)

and

> Now it came to pass in those days that He
> went out to the mountain to pray, and continued
> all night in prayer to God. (Luke 6:12)

We should be seeking the kingdom of God as we would a great treasure, as Jesus did, before and during each choice we make. We should choose to follow Jesus and seek God at the beginning of the day, as said in Mark 1:35. And we should pray before making important decisions, as Jesus did in Luke 6:12 before He chose His disciples.

To Submit and to Resist

I have heard it said many, many times that if you resist the devil, he will flee from you. I have resisted the devil, and he has fled from me. But I also have resisted the devil, and he has stayed where he was. What was the difference in my resisting that caused the devil to flee or not to flee? Let us take a look at James 4:7.

> Submit yourselves therefore to God. Resist
> the devil, and he will flee from you. (James 4:7)

The answer is in the submitting in the first part of the verse. There were times when I chose to submit, and there were times when I chose not to submit. Now, when I hear a man or woman of God say how they resisted the devil, and he fled, I know that they also submitted to God. They stay in a state of submission. We should also stay in a state of submission.

Submitting and resisting are similar to a coin. A coin such as a quarter has a head side and a tail side. Submitting is the head side, and resisting is the tail side. However, many people, including myself, sometimes want to focus on the backside of the coin. They want to resist the devil so that he will flee. Others want only to submit to God, and they wonder why the devil is still there. But the promise of God occurs when we choose to submit to Him and resist the devil. You need the whole coin, not just one side of the coin. What does it mean to submit and to resist?

We submit when we subordinate ourselves to God by humbling ourselves before God and obeying God. Humbling yourself before God is recognizing that the Father, Son, and Holy Spirit are God and that you are not. That means we give God control over our lives. The action of submitting is obedience. Obeying is simply choosing to follow instructions. When God says to build an ark, you build it—without questions.

Resisting the devil means standing against or opposing the devil. We are to be in opposition to the devil's desires. We are not in opposition when we close our eyes to sin or tolerate or negotiate with evil. Jesus didn't negotiate with people selling goods in the temple. He made a whip and chased them out.

The first significant act of submitting is when you became born-again. Making Jesus Lord of your life. Keeping Jesus as the Lord of your life is what we must choose to do every day. Jesus being Lord of your life means that you willingly give control of your life to Jesus. I have seen bumper stickers on cars saying, "Jesus is my co-pilot." I never understood that saying. Jesus should be our pilot. I want the person who only wants what is best for me (Jeremiah 29:11) and knows the end from the beginning (Isaiah 46:10) to be in charge of my life. Submitting to God also means that you must obey what He says to do. Your thought might be, *But I don't hear God speaking.* God is always speaking to you through the Holy Spirit.

You must get accustomed to hearing Him. I can be in a group of people, with many conversations going on, and can say my wife's name, and she will look over at me. My wife knows my voice, and I know her voice. For example, you are a mother or a father, and you are at a playground with lots of kids playing and making noise, and you are in a conversation with other parents. Yet if you hear a child crying, you immediately know if it is your child crying. You know your child's voice. We are to know God's voice like we know the voice of a child, a wife, or a husband. First Kings 19:12 informs us that God's voice is a still, small voice. In John 10:27, Jesus tells us, "My sheep hear My voice, and I know them, and they follow Me."

There is also the written Word of God, the Bible. The number one thing you need to obey is the Word of God. God instructs His people through His Word. The Bible is written to you and is God telling you how you are to live. God gives you examples of what to do in different situations and how He deals with people who follow His Word and people that reject His Word. However, to obey God's Word, it will be necessary for you to read and study the Bible. Listening to others teach about the Scriptures will help your understanding of what you are reading and studying, but you need to be able to feed yourself. Submitting to God requires choosing to obey the Scriptures.

Summiting to God also means humbling yourself to God. We humble ourselves through prayer and worship. Prayer indicates that you recognize that God is greater than you, and you desire a relationship with Him. Worshiping God also recognizes that He is greater than you and that you place Him above everything and everyone else. Humbling, worshiping, praying, reading, studying, listening, and obeying God are all choices that you have to make. But it is also essential that you choose to resist.

When reading the Bible, you will find many examples of how different people resisted the devil. We are disciples of Jesus, so let's take an example of Him resisting the devil from the fourth chapter of Matthew.

> v. 1 Then Jesus was led up by the Spirit into the wilderness to be tempted by the devil.
>
> v. 2 And when He had fasted forty days and forty nights, afterward He was hungry.
>
> v. 3 Now when the tempter came to Him, he said, "If You are the Son of God, command that these stones become bread."
>
> v. 4 But He answered and said, "It is written, 'MAN SHALL NOT LIVE BY BREAD ALONE, BUT BY EVERY WORD THAT PROCEEDS FROM THE MOUTH OF GOD.'"
>
> v. 5 Then the devil took Him up into the holy city, set Him on the pinnacle of the temple,
>
> v. 6 and said to Him, "If You are the Son of God, throw Yourself down. For it is written: 'HE SHALL GIVE HIS ANGELS CHARGE OVER YOU,' and,

IN THEIR HANDS THEY SHALL BEAR YOU UP, LEST YOU DASH YOUR FOOT AGAINST A STONE.'"

v. 7 Jesus said to him, "It is written again, 'YOU SHALL NOT TEMPT THE LORD YOUR GOD.'"

v. 8 Again, the devil took Him up on an exceedingly high mountain, and showed Him all the kingdoms of the world and their glory.

v. 9 And he said to Him, "All these things I will give You if You will fall down and worship me."

v. 10 Then Jesus said to him, "Away with you, Satan! For it is written, 'YOU SHALL WORSHIP THE LORD YOUR GOD, AND HIM ONLY YOU SHALL SERVE.'"

v. 11 Then the devil left Him, and behold, angels came and ministered to Him. (Matthew 4:1–11)

The first two verses set the stage for what is about to happen. The *then* in verse 1 referred to chapter 3 when John the Baptist baptized Jesus, and God confirmed that Jesus was His Son and that God was pleased with Jesus. Verse 1 tells us that Jesus was led by the Spirit to be tempted by the devil. Then in verse 2, we are told that after, He went into the wilderness and fasted for forty days and nights. I call that unwaveringly submitted. Then the verse says that Jesus was hungry. After fasting forty days and nights, saying that Jesus was hungry is an understatement. Then in verses 3, 6, and 9, the devil gives his temptations to Jesus. Jesus resists the devil in each of these temptations by quoting the written Word of God. Each time Jesus opposes the devil by choosing to tell the devil what the scriptures said about the situation, which requires knowing the Word of God and standing firm on its truth. Choose to get God's Word deep in your heart so that your first response is God's Word when the devil attacks. Then you will be able to tell the devil what God says about the situation.

Another example of resisting the devil is in Genesis 39, where Joseph chose to run away from Potiphar's wife.

> v. 11 But it happened about this time, when Joseph went into the house to do his work, and none of the men of the house *was* inside,
> v. 12 that she caught him by his garment, saying, "Lie with me." But he left his garment in her hand, and fled and ran outside. (Genesis 39:11–12)

Verse 11 starts with "But it happened about this time." The statement tells me that this was not the norm for Joseph to go into the house to work when no other men were there. But it happened this time. His desire was not to be alone with Potiphar's wife. His choice would have been for others to be in the house. Sometimes when you are avoiding a situation, that situation can happen anyway. Joseph decided the best course of action was to flee the entrapment that the devil had set before him. Even though Joseph resisted Potiphar's wife, it appeared that the devil had won. But God turned it into good, and he eventually became the second most powerful man in the world.

The examples of Jesus and Joseph resisting the devil indicate two different ways of resisting the devil. You can resist by speaking as Jesus did or through steps of action like Joseph. It shows that we can resist the devil supernaturally and/or naturally. Jesus spoke the Word of God, which is Spirit and life. Joseph physically ran from Potiphar's wife, a natural action.

The important thing is choosing to submit to God and resist the devil. Both Jesus and Joseph were submitted to God and resisted the devil in the accounts discussed. Jesus was always submitted to the Father. In Luke 4:10, Jesus told the devil to go away, and the devil left Jesus. Luke 4:13 says that the devil "departed from Him until an opportune time." It tells me that the devil may depart from you, but he has not given up. Because the devil never gives up, we should always be submitted to God and ready to resist the devil. Joseph showed his submission when he said to Potiphar's wife in Genesis 39:9, "How then can I do this great wickedness, and sin against God?" When the devil tempts you, make sure that you submit to God and resist the devil, and the devil will flee.

To Guard Your Heart

The choice of guarding your heart might be the most crucial choice you make after being born-again. Renewing our minds to the things of God is critical. However, if you continue allowing the things of this world that are contrary to God's Word to enter your heart, they will counterbalance God's Word. I know that this has been true in my life. I believe that the lack of guarding one's heart is common among most Christians.

Whenever God tells you to do something, you will have to choose to obey or disobey. The determining factor of whether you obey or disobey is what is in your heart. Your heart is where your spirit (the real you) and your soul (your mind, will, and emotions) intersect. As you can see, I am not talking about your physical heart. You are a spirit that has a soul that lives in a body. To better understand this truth, I suggest you read *Spirit, Soul and Body*, written by Andrew Wommack.

When you were born-again, your spirit man was made brand-new. Your body remained as it was. Your soul also remained the same but now can be renewed by renewing your mind. Your spirit was made brand-new through your spirit and Jesus's Spirit becoming one spirit, which eliminated the sin infection. Because of your renewed spirit, there became dissonance in your heart between your spirit and your soul. Of these two elements, the spirit and soul, the one that is dominant controls your body. It's like a scale similar to the Scales of Justice. However, your born-again spirit and your soul are never in a state of balance in your heart. On the right side of the scale, you have your born-again spirit, which was made perfect and sealed to remain perfect. On the left side of the scale is your soul (your mind, will, and emotions), programmed by a fallen and ungodly world. As the weight on one side of the scale increases, that side increases in control, and the other side decreases in control. Luke chapter 6 speaks of what I am discussing.

> v. 43 For a good tree does not bear bad fruit, nor does a bad tree bear good fruit.
> v. 44 For every tree is known by its own fruit. For *men* do not gather figs from thorns, nor do they gather grapes from a bramble bush.
> v. 45 A good man out of the good treasure of his heart brings forth good; and an evil man out of the evil treasure of his heart brings forth evil. For out of the abundance of the heart his mouth speaks. (Luke 6:43–45)

Here in the first two verses, Jesus is talking about trees. He lets us know that a tree's fruit tells you what type of tree you are observing. Only by observing the fruit will you know the kind of tree. Jesus talked about gathering figs and thorns and grapes and bramblebushes. I will discuss apples and cherries. I grew up in Michigan, where they have apple and cherry orchards. I have never gone to a cherry orchard to pick apples. Your thought probably is that nobody would ever do that. Verse 45 tells us that a good man will bring forth good things, and an evil man will bring forth evil things. Often I find people going to a cherry orchard to pick apples. I say that because I find people expecting an evil person to do good things. You must guard your heart because it will determine whether you will do good things or evil things, and people will know what type of person you are by what you do. In Proverbs chapter 4, Solomon instructs his son in wisdom by giving his son instructions on guarding his heart.

> v. 20 My son, give attention to my words;
> Incline your ear to my sayings.
> v. 21 Do not let them depart from your eyes; Keep them in the midst of your heart;

v. 22 For they *are* life to those who find them, And health to all their flesh.

v. 23 Keep your heart with all diligence, For out of it *spring* the issues of life.

v. 24 Put away from you a deceitful mouth, And put perverse lips far from you.

v. 25 Let your eyes look straight ahead, And your eyelids look right before you.

v. 26 Ponder the path of your feet, And let all your ways be established.

v. 27 Do not turn to the right or the left; Remove your foot from evil. (Proverbs 4:20–27)

When I read these verses, I hear God telling me always to give attention to God's written Word, what the Holy Spirit is telling me, and what other people are instructing me about God's Word. God tells me not to depart from His Word and keep His Word the most important thing in my heart. Most of all, God is telling me to protect my heart from the evil of this world because my heart will determine my life. God is saying not to speak evil things or allow my eyes to focus on the evil around me. I should always consider what I am doing and where I am going. I am to follow God's directions, and if I find myself off God's path, I am to get back on God's path quickly.

From these verses, I see three gateways to our hearts. These gateways are what we see, hear, and say. I am now going to date myself. Remember when you were a kid, and they had three monkeys sitting in a row. The monkeys were "see no evil," "speak no evil," and "hear no evil." To guard our hearts, we need to choose to see no evil, speak no evil, and hear no evil. What your eyes focus on, what you speak, and what you constantly hear is implanted in your heart.

The first part of Proverbs 23:7 says, "For as he thinks in his heart, so is he." So what you think is what you are. This is exciting stuff. The verse means your life is what it is because of what you have seen, heard, and said in the past. That means that you can control your future by controlling what you see, hear, and speak today. To become the man or woman that God wants you to become, you must choose to read the Bible, hear ministers teaching about God's Word, listen to the revelations of the Word given to you via the Holy Spirit, and speak the truths in the Bible. Isn't it fantastic that your life is dependent on what you choose to see, hear, and speak?

To Be a Disciple

If you have chosen to make Jesus your Lord and Savior by being born-again, you have started your journey with Christ. After making that life-altering choice, you should choose to become a disciple of Jesus. Often the born-again experience is the focal point of the great commission. Below is Matthew 28:16–20, which are the verses of the great commission.

> v. 16 Then the eleven disciples went away into Galilee, to the mountain which Jesus had appointed for them.
> v. 17 When they saw Him, they worshiped Him; but some doubted.
> v. 18 And Jesus came and spoke to them, saying, "All authority has been given to Me in heaven and on earth.
> v. 19 Go therefore and make disciples of all the nations, baptizing them in the name of the Father and of the Son and of the Holy Spirit,
> v. 20 teaching them to observe all things that I have commanded you; and lo, I am with you always, *even* to the end of the age." Amen. (Matthew 28:16–20)

In these verses, Jesus is telling the disciples to go and make more disciples. In verse 18, Jesus informs us that He now has all authority in heaven and earth. It means that Jesus now possesses the authority Adam and Eve gave to the devil. What I find most interesting in verses 19 and 20 is Jesus didn't say for the disciples to go and make converts. Jesus tells them to teach and baptize and do all He had commanded to others. You teach and baptize those that are already converted. Today the emphasis is on converting people. That is to get people out of the kingdom of darkness into the kingdom of light, which is getting people born-again. Being converted is the first step, but it is not the endgame. If you are only a born-again believer, you still need to grow in your knowledge of the Word and your relationship with Jesus to be the most effective. When people join the military, they are not put into a battle without training or equipment. A soldier is given extensive training and the best equipment possible before being sent into battle. When a person is born-again, they may at once find themselves in a battle. Because their spirit man has been made new with the Holy Spirit, they have the weapons for the battle. But they need their mind renewed with the Word of God to know what they have and how it is to be used.

The martial arts are an example of discipleship. You go to a dojo and sign the contract to become a member of the dojo. Signing the contract made you a member of the dojo, not a follower or disciple of the sensei. Just like going to church doesn't make you a born-again believer. To be a disciple of the sensei, you have to start training under the sensei. In most martial arts, you start as a white belt and progress through different color belts until you earn your black belt. The obtaining of the different belts is not based on how long you have been training but on how well you have mastered the required skills. You can choose to train once a week, once a month, or once a day. The more often you train, the faster you acquire the skills and progress to your black belt. Most people join the dojo and have their *gi* and white belt, but no more. Many years ago, I joined a dojo. I had the gi and the white belt and trained for a couple of months. Then I had an injury and stopped. I didn't spend enough time with the sensei to master the skills the sensei was teaching. The same can be said of Christians. It isn't how long you have been a believer that makes you mature but to what extent you have renewed your mind to the Word of God. Most believers have not progressed past the beginning stage of discipleship. Discipleship grows out of a relationship, and they have not taken time to grow in their relationship with Jesus, to learn who they are in Christ and what God has commanded and promised them. To do these things, they must adhere to Romans 12:2.

> And do not be conformed to this world, but be transformed by the renewing of your mind, that you may prove what *is* that good and acceptable and perfect will of God. (Romans 12:2)

To grow in your relationship with Jesus, you need to learn who you are in Christ and know what God has promised. In martial arts, you are training to become a black belt. As you grow in your relationship with Jesus, you will discover yourself developing into a stronger and more mature disciple. That is why as a born-again believer, you must study God's Word to renew your mind. As you renew your mind, your relationship with our triune God will increase, your identity of who you are in Christ will grow, and you will clearly understand what God has promised you. In martial arts, not everyone becomes a black belt, but everyone has the opportunity to become a black belt. Just as everyone has the opportunity to become a mature disciple of Jesus, but many will not. It's your choice. God has given every born-again believer the measure of His Spirit. But we must grow into the knowledge of what we have. We continually need to renew our minds to the things of God.

Every born-again believer can be a disciple. Because you can become a disciple of Jesus, it is important to know what He said about what it takes to be one of His disciples. Jesus tells us we must love Him and forsake our love for everything else to be His disciple. Look at what Jesus tells us in Luke 14:26–27.

> v. 26 If anyone comes to Me and does not hate his father and mother, wife and children, brothers and sisters, yes, and his own life also, he cannot be My disciple.
>
> v. 27 And whoever does not bear his cross and come after Me cannot be My disciple. (Luke 14:26–27)

Jesus said, "If anyone come to Me, and does not hate." We know we have to love Jesus to follow after Jesus. This verse tells us we must hate our family and even ourself to love Jesus. This hate is not hatred, as most tend to think of hate. But a level of importance. Your love for Jesus must be far above your love for any person or thing. You have a love for your family and yourself, which must be below your love for Jesus. If you don't place your love for Jesus above your love for other things, including family, friends, and yourself, you can't be a disciple of Jesus.

In verse 27, Jesus said that you could not be His disciple if you don't endure what this world will throw at you because you are a follower of Jesus. This theme expressed in verses 26 and 27 is also in Matthew 16:24 and Luke 14:33.

> Then Jesus said to His disciples, "If anyone desires to come after Me, let him deny himself, and take up his cross, and follow Me." (Matthew 16:24)

and

> So likewise, whoever of you does not forsake all that he has cannot be My disciple. (Luke 14:33)

Again, in these two verses, Jesus says that we must place Him above everything else. Matthew 16:24 reads very similar to Luke 14:27, with the addition of denying ourselves. Denying ourselves is to deny our will and identity that we have developed living in this world. Our desire should be to replace our will, with Jesus's will, in our lives. Also, our identity must become the identity that we have in Jesus Christ. Luke 14:33 says that we must forsake all we have to be His disciple. In this verse, all means all. That is, Jesus's place in our lives is superior to and more important than all people and all things. In chess, your king is the most valuable piece to you. All the pieces have value, and some pieces have more value than others. Jesus is our

King. He is more valuable to us than any other person or thing on this earth. Other people and things have value to us. But Jesus has the greatest value of all.

One of the most valuable things that Jesus has given us is His Word. John 8:31 and 32 indicate the value of Jesus's Word.

> v. 31 Then Jesus said to those Jews who believed Him, "If you abide in My word, you are My disciples indeed.
> v. 32 And you shall know the truth, and the truth shall make you free." (John 8:31–32)

Here in verse 31, we are told that if you continue in, remain in, and not depart from Jesus's Word, then you truly are a disciple of Jesus. Joshua 1:8 tells us to speak God's Word, meditate in God's Word day and night, and do all that is in the Word.

> This Book of the Law shall not depart from your mouth, but you shall meditate in it day and night, that you may observe to do according to all that is written in it. For then you will make your way prosperous, and then you will have good success. (Joshua 1:8)

In this verse, we are told not to stop speaking the Word of God, meditate on the Word of God day and night, and watch to make sure we do all that is in the Word of God. Speaking, meditating, and doing the Word of God is genuinely abiding in God's Word. The wonderful thing about abiding in the Word is that it will set you free from the worldly passions that have enslaved you and prove that you are truly a disciple of Jesus.

CHAPTER 6

You Get to Choose (Part 2)

Your Identity

Who you think you are and what you think you are will make a difference in your choices. If you believe that man evolved from other forms of animals, you have identified yourself as only an animal. If you think that you are only an animal, you have neglected the spirit that God breathed into you, and you will live only in the natural realm. Because you only live in the natural realm, you will not be able to overcome the lusts of the flesh. But man didn't evolve from apes or any other animal. So what is man? Man is the special creation of God. Genesis 1:27 tells us that man was created in the image and likeness of God. When God created animals, He spoke them into existence. But in Genesis 2:7, we are told that God formed man, and He breathed life into man.

> And the LORD God formed man *of* the dust
> of the ground, and breathed into his nostrils the
> breath of life; and man became a living being.
> (Genesis 2:7)

The breath of life that God breathed into man was His Spirit. So man is the only creature God created in His image and likeness and has His Spirit.

God gave man the authority over the earth. Then man gave the authority God gave him to the devil. God sent His only begotten Son to save man from that misguided choice.

> v. 16 For God so loved the world that He gave His only begotten Son, that whoever believes in Him should not perish but have everlasting life.
> v. 17 For God did not send His Son into the world to condemn the world, but that the world through Him might be saved.
> v. 18 "He who believes in Him is not condemned; but he who does not believe is condemned already, because he has not believed in the name of the only begotten Son of God."
> (John 3:16–18)

These scriptures explain that God loved the world that He created and sent His Son to save man, whom God had given authority over the world. Through Jesus, God gave man the opportunity for salvation. However, we only receive salvation when we believe in the only begotten Son of God. When we receive salvation, we are adopted into the family of God and become children of God. It is known as being *born-again*. When your spirit is renewed with Jesus's Spirit. When you're born-again, the spiritual identity of who you are is changed. There is a new you.

One of the things that change when you are born-again is your motivation. The basis of how this world motivates differs from how God motivates. Have you ever been to a motivational seminar? I have been to many. My entire working career after college was in sales. There are many meetings with a career in sales, and some of those meetings will have a motivational session. Also, my wife and I have tried working on a couple of multilevel product programs, and they are always attempting to motivate you. In motivational and success seminars, one thing that is stressed is your *why* for what you are doing. The idea is that your why is what will motivate you to succeed. Your why is your purpose or reason for doing what you are doing. Your why is important, but the essential thing is who you are. Who you are relates to your identity. For example, an apple tree produces apples not because it decided to produce apples and not pears. But because it is an apple tree. Its identity is as an apple tree, and because it is an apple tree, it produces apples. If you are born-again, you have the fruit of the Spirit. In Galatians 5:22–23, the fruit of the Spirit is detailed.

> v. 22 But the fruit of the Spirit is love, joy,
> peace, longsuffering, gentleness, goodness, faith,
> v. 23 Meekness, temperance: against such
> there is no law. (Galatians 5:22–23)

Like the apple, these fruits should manifest in your life. Not because you have to force them out, but because that is who you are. As your identification with Jesus increases, these fruits will increasingly manifest in your life.

Who you are will determine your definition of success. The more your identity is in Christ, the more your definition of success will differ from the world's definition. As a believer in Jesus, success is finding and fulfilling God's will for your life. The world's definition of success involves how much money you have, how big a star or public figure you can become, or how much status you have. A believer's definition of success should not be having lots of money, being very well-known, or being the most important person. For a believer, if you are not fulfilling God's plan for your life, you have not been successful. The believer's definition of success becomes fulfilling their God-given mission here on earth. This way, they will choose activities that lead to fulfilling that mission. Who you are is wrapped up in your identity. The more you choose to identify with Christ, the more your choices will be determined by that identification.

Our identity in Christ leads us into a discussion on spirit, soul, and body. Just as God is a three-part being—Father, Son, and Holy Spirit—we are also a three-part being. First Thessalonians 5:23 tells us what we are.

Now may the God of peace Himself sanctify you completely; and may your whole spirit, soul, and body be preserved blameless at the coming of our Lord Jesus Christ. (1 Thessalonians 5:23)

This verse says that we are spirit, soul, and body. We are a spirit that has a soul and lives in a body. Until we were born-again, the natural world programmed our spirit. Our soul is the interface between the spirit and the body. Our flesh, which relates to the natural world, is our body. Our spirit and body give us a natural and spiritual component to our identity. We have to choose to walk in our spiritual identity in Christ. Here is what Galatians 5:16–17 says about our spiritual walk.

v. 16 I say then: Walk in the Spirit, and you shall not fulfill the lust of the flesh.

v. 17 For the flesh lusts against the Spirit, and the Spirit against the flesh; and these are contrary to one another, so that you do not do the things that you wish. (Galatians 5:16–17)

Here is the AMPC version of Galatians 5:16–17.

v. 16 But I say, walk *and* live [*habitually*] in the [*Holy*] Spirit [*responsive to and controlled and guided by the Spirit*]; then you will certainly not gratify the cravings *and* desires of the flesh (of human nature without God).

v. 17 For the desires of the flesh are opposed to the [*Holy*] Spirit, and the [*desires of the*] Spirit are opposed to the flesh (godless human nature); for these are antagonistic to each other [*continually withstanding and in conflict with each other*], so that you are not free *but* are prevented from doing what you desire to do. (Galatians 5:16–17 AMPC)

This is how I read Galatians 5:16.

> I say then: Walk in your spiritual identity,
> and you shall not fulfill the strong forbidden
> desires of your fleshly identity.

Galatians 5:16 tells us that if we walk in the spirit, we will not walk after the flesh. I have heard people say that the way to be spiritual is to control our flesh. I have tried, and you most likely have tried to control your flesh to be spiritual. But that doesn't work. This verse says that if you don't want to fulfill your fleshly desires, you have to choose to follow after your spiritual identity in Jesus Christ. As we focus on walking in our identity in Christ and not our fleshly identity, we will walk more and more in our identity in Jesus. Verse 17 shows an even stronger conflict between our Christian and fleshly identities. This verse informs us that our fleshly identity is opposed to our identity in Christ. They are so opposed to each other that they are at war against each other. We can't fight the war against our fleshly desires without knowing our identity in Jesus Christ.

We must come to the knowledge of who we are in the spirit the same way as Jesus. Jesus didn't learn who He was from His mother, Mary. The Bible tells us that she pondered the things concerning Jesus in her own heart. She did not tell Jesus who He was. Being faithful Jews, I am sure that Joseph and Mary took Jesus and His brothers and sisters to the temple every Saturday. Because the seed implanted into Mary came from the Word of God, Jesus's Spirit was not compromised by sin. Not having a sinful nature allowed Jesus to hear the Holy Spirit. Here is what Luke 2:40 says about Jesus.

> And the Child grew and became strong in
> spirit, filled with wisdom; and the grace of God
> was upon Him. (Luke 2:40)

Here we are told that the Child (Jesus) not only grew physically but that He grew in spirit and wisdom. Also, we are told that the grace of God was on Him. He grew in spirit, wisdom, and grace because the Holy Spirit spoke to Him through the scriptures that He heard from His parents and at the temple. Jesus showed that He was aware of who He was at twelve years old when He stayed behind in Jerusalem as the family returned home to Nazareth. When Joseph and Mary determined that Jesus was not in the group returning to Nazareth, they returned to Jerusalem to find Him. Luke 2:48–50 tells us what happened when they found Jesus.

> v. 48 So when they saw Him, they were amazed; and His mother said to Him, "Son, why have You done this to us? Look, Your father and I have sought You anxiously."
> v. 49 And He said to them, "Why did you seek Me? Did you not know that I must be about My Father's business?" (Luke 2:48–49)

Verse 49 tells us that at twelve years of age, Jesus knew His purpose here on earth. We, as born-again believers, also need to fulfill our purpose and perform our Father's business. That purpose will only be fulfilled by knowing who we are in the spirit and what we have been given through our relationship with Jesus. This will require the transformation of our thinking as noted in Romans 12:2.

> And do not be conformed to this world, but be transformed by the renewing of your mind, that you may prove what *is* that good and acceptable and perfect will of God. (Romans 12:2)

The verse informs us that we are to change our mind from a worldly mindset to a Christ-centered mindset. As we change to a Christ-centered mindset, we will come to know God's good, acceptable, and perfect will for our life, causing us to no longer conform to the ways of this evil world. A picture of what hearing and meditating on God's Word does is in James 1:23–25.

> v. 23 For if any be a hearer of the word, and
> not a doer, he is like unto a man beholding his
> natural face in a glass:
> v. 24 For he beholdeth himself, and goeth
> his way, and straightway forgetteth what manner
> of man he was.
> v. 25 But whoso looketh into the perfect law
> of liberty, and continueth *therein,* he being not a
> forgetful hearer, but a doer of the work, this man
> shall be blessed in his deed. (James 1:23–25)

These verses describe God's Word as a mirror. Meditating on the Word is compared to looking into a mirror. If you are like me, when you get up in the morning, one of the first things you do is go to the bathroom and look at yourself in the mirror. What you are looking at is your physical identity. Have you ever begun to leave the house and had to go back to that mirror to make sure of how you look? I have. You and I can forget who we are in the spirit. Because of our forgetfulness, we must continue looking into the Word of God, our spiritual mirror, to know who we are in our born-again spirit.

When you were born again, you received all these fruits even if you don't think you have.

There are many other examples in the Bible of the mighty works accomplished by people that embraced their godly identity. There is David, who killed a lion and a bear after he was anointed to be the next king of Israel. I know that the Bible didn't give the chronological order in David's life when he killed the lion and the bear. But I believe that in 1 Samuel 17:34–37, when David told Saul about killing the lion and the bear, he was reminding himself of what he had performed after being anointed to be the next king. Then he went out under that anointing and killed Goliath. Moses's godly identity was with the Hebrew people and his belief that he was to free his people from the rule of Egypt. Moses eventually led his Hebrew brothers and sisters from Egypt after he humbled himself and fol-lowed God's plan. My favorite identity change in the Bible is Saul, who became known as Paul. Saul's identity changed from being the strictest of Hebrews in following the law to becoming a disciple of Jesus Christ. When Saul changed his spiritual identity and became a disciple of Jesus, he became known as Paul and wrote most of the New Testament. If you are born-again, your spirit is one with Jesus's Spirit, and your identity should be centered on who you are in Jesus Christ. You also need to go forth every day and be your true identity.

Your Friends

You get to select your friends, and those friends will influence your choices. You can't always select the pool of people from which you will select your friends. For example, I was nine years old when my family moved from Muskegon, Michigan, to North Muskegon, Michigan. That doesn't sound like a big move. But I had to change schools from Froebel to Reeths-Puffer. For me, a fourth-grader, that was a huge change. I was in a new environment and had to find or, should I say, choose new friends. Other than my relatives that attended Froebel, I never saw any of those friends again. The pool of kids I could select friends from changed from one neighborhood and school to another neighborhood and school. I am not sure what difference in influence the change of friends made in my life, but I trust my parents moved for the betterment of the whole family. But I did have to choose new friends. I didn't know it at that time, but who you select as friends affects your life. Your friends can be a blessing or a curse. Psalm 1:1 gives a unique perspective on how the right friends can bless you.

> v. 1 Blessed *is* the man Who walks not in the counsel of the ungodly, Nor stands in the path of sinners, Nor sits in the seat of the scornful. (Psalm 1:1)

These verses tell us if the people you do life with are godly, righteous, and loving, you are blessed. This verse also means that you are not blessed if the people you do life with are ungodly, sinners, or scornful. Let's read what 1 Corinthians 15:33 says regarding the influence that your friendships have.

> Do not be deceived: "Evil company corrupts good habits." (1 Corinthians 15:33)

This verse reveals that people can be deceived about the effects people they spend time with have on their behavior. The verse also informs us that if we are around people that have bad habits and do things that are not good, we will find one day ourselves having bad habits and that we will be doing wrong things. The contrast is that if we are around people with good habits and that do good things, we will have good habits and do good things.

Because of the influence friends have on children, parents attempt to manage their children's friends. Parents select the pool from which their children can choose friends by selecting their neighborhood and the school they attend. Even after managing the group that their children can choose friends from, they may find undesirables. That is why parents tell their children to avoid some children. Unfortunately, parents sometimes think children that would be great for their children as friends are bad for their children. One task of parents is to instruct their children on how to choose friends.

Proverbs, the book of wisdom, guides our selection of friends. Here are a few examples of that guidance.

> The righteous should choose his friends carefully, For the way of the wicked leads them astray. (Proverbs 12:26)

> He who walks with wise *men* will be wise, But the companion of fools will be destroyed. (Proverbs 13:20)

> Make no friendship with an angry man, And with a furious man do not go, Lest you learn

his ways And set a snare for your soul. (Proverbs
22:24–25)

These verses inform us that if you want to live righteously and
wise, your friends can't be wicked, foolish, angry, or furious because
you will learn the ways of your friends. As believers in Christ, we
are to be the example. The world is not to be our example. In 1
Corinthians 11:1, Paul tells us he is to be our example.

Imitate me, just as I also *imitate* Christ. (1
Corinthians 11:1)

Paul is relaying that a believer can be our example as long as that
person makes Christ their example. Looking a step deeper into this
statement, we see that Christ is always to be our example. Because
Christ is our first example, the person we are following is a second
example. There are times believers want an example that is physically
present, but we should only follow them as they follow Christ. Third
John 1:11 gives us another viewpoint.

Beloved, do not imitate what is evil, but
what is good. He who does good is of God, but
he who does evil has not seen God. (3 John 1:11)

John informs us not to imitate or make our example those
who are evil. The reason not to imitate evil people is that they don't
have an accurate concept of God and will eventually lead us to evil
behavior.

There is one other thing about interaction with unbelievers.
You can't be the light to this dark world without interacting with
unbelievers. As believers, we need to make sure that we influence
unbelievers and that they are not influencing us. One way you can
protect yourself from being influenced by the darkness of this world
is to choose to follow Hebrews 10:24–25.

> v. 24 And let us consider one another in order to stir up love and good works,
>
> v. 25 not forsaking the assembling of ourselves together, as *is* the manner of some, but exhorting *one another,* and so much the more as you see the Day approaching. (Hebrews 10:24–25)

Verse 24 gives an important reason we should have Christian friends. We should have Christian friends to encourage one another to perform good works. Verse 25 tells us not to forsake the assembling or gathering together with each other. This verse is often used to tell believers that they should not forsake going to church. And that is true. But I believe that it also speaks to the fact that we should choose to gather together with other believers in everyday life activities. It is good when we can form relationships with other believers while at work. But we can also take those relationships that we develop at church and work into deeper personal relationships. For example, recently, we had good Christian friends from Pennsylvania visit us in Florida. It was enjoyable and encouraging catching up with each other. Visits like this are great fun and uplifting.

But as followers of Christ, we must interact with believers and unbelievers. When you review the life of Jesus, most of the people He met didn't believe who He was when they first met Him. But they soon came to believe that He was the Son of God. We aren't going to have unbelievers become believers without interaction with them. Proverbs 27:17 indicates what type of interaction we are to have with our believing and unbelieving friends.

> *As* iron sharpens iron, So a man sharpens the countenance of his friend. (Proverbs 27:17)

We are being told in this verse that whether the friends we choose are believers or unbelievers, we are to make them better, and they should make you better. In athletics, friends train together to push each other to greater accomplishments. The most important way to sharpen a friend is to improve their knowledge, understanding, and walk with Jesus. Choose friends that will sharpen your relationship with God and that you can help sharpen their relationship with God. But remember that everybody has free will. You can't make your friends accept Jesus as Lord and Savior. You can only tell them your story and what God's Word says.

I started the section by talking about how you get to choose your friends. But we see two very important aspects of having a friend in Proverbs chapter 18.

> A man *who has* friends must himself be
> friendly, But there is a friend *who* sticks closer
> than a brother. (Proverbs 18:24)

The first part of this verse informs us what we must do to have friends. We must be friendly. We all know people that are annoying and not pleasant to be around. Those are the people who don't have many, if any, friends. But if you want to have friends, you have to choose to be friendly. Being friendly might mean you have to speak first to someone or invite people to your house. It could mean going out of your way to help someone.

The second part of the verse indicates why having friends can be important. We all have the opportunity to encounter tough times. It could be the loss of a loved one, the loss of a job, or the discovery of an illness. Tough times can come in many degrees. But in those tough times, it can be beneficial to have a friend that will listen to you and encourage you. The verse tells us that a good friend will stick by your side better than a relative. So when choosing friends, choose well, for they will impact your life.

Your Plans

Planning is a powerful tool to make sure your choices are the choices you want to make. For example, you have to be at work at 7:00 a.m., and you know that it will take you twenty minutes to drive to work and thirty minutes to get ready to go to work. So you set your alarm clock for 6:00 a.m. to give yourself a ten-minute grace period. By setting the alarm for 6:00 a.m., you have planned what time you will get out of bed. A second option would have been to go to bed and hope you will wake up in time. Say you chose the second option and wake up at 6:40 a.m. Getting up at 6:40 a.m. was not the choice you wanted to make. You now must rush to get out of the house to arrive on time, after that twenty-minute drive to work. You rush and get out of the house at 6:50 a.m., and you are now going to be ten minutes late to work. How often can you be ten or more minutes late for work and keep your job? So you speed to get to work on time, and the police pull you over and issue you a speeding ticket. Now not only are you very late, you also have to pay for the ticket. It could have been worse. Instead of the speeding ticket, you could have been in an accident, which would have caused even greater problems for you.

Planning, as we have seen, can keep you out of trouble. Planning also helps maintain things in a proper sequence so things work smoothly. An excellent example of how the proper sequences make things work better is Genesis chapter 1, when God created this world from an earth that was without form, void and dark.

Day 1—God created light and separated the light from the darkness. Then He called the light "day" and the dark "night".

Day 2—God made the firmament and divided the waters under the firmament from the waters above the firmament.

Day 3—God separated the waters from the land, and then He created grass, herb seeds, and fruit trees.

Day 4—God created the sun and moon to separate day and night. They were created for signs, seasons, days, and years. He also created the stars on the fourth day.

Day 5—God created the creatures of the water and the fowl of the air.

Day 6—God created the beasts of the earth and man. Man was created in the image and likeness of God and given authority over everything God had created on the earth.

The sequence of creation was critical. If man was created before there was land, he would have had to have been a great swimmer. If he were created before trees, man would have to dodge trees as they sprung out of the ground. The fascinating part about creation was that God created light before He created the sun, moon, and stars. This sequence brings many questions to mind. For example, what would have happened if God created the sun and stars and said for them to radiate light. Would that eliminate any other thing from emitting light? That would mean no light bulbs or candlelight dinners. God planned the sequence of how He created the earth, and we should be thankful for it.

Let's look at another aspect of planning. My wife and I have built two homes. This process involves many choices. We started by choosing how we wanted the house to look and function from our memory of homes we have lived in or have visited. The memory of past homes and the inspection of the builder's current homes helped us choose the things we would want in our new home. And at the same time, this process gave us information on what we would not want in our new home. Next, we worked with the builder to select the building plans for the house and the list of the building products that we wanted in the house. This process can take several revisions because they may not fit together as we believed they would when looking at our choices. The next step in the process is the signing of the contract. The builder's contract will normally include a clause stating how much changes in the contract will cost the homeowner. This clause is because during the home's construction, the homeowner may decide that they don't like how their choices are coming together and desire to make changes.

In our discussion of building a home, you can see that when planning, writing down the choices you have determined is a good thing. Writing down your choices helps you to clarify your options. Clarified choices give you and others the direction for what is to accomplish. God talks about writing down your plan in Habakkuk 2:2–3.

> v. 2 Then the LORD answered me and said:
> "Write the vision And make *it* plain on tablets,
> That he may run who reads it.
>
> v. 3 For the vision *is* yet for an appointed
> time; But at the end it will speak, and it will not
> lie. Though it tarries, wait for it; Because it will
> surely come, It will not tarry." (Habakkuk 2:2–3)

I know that these scriptures are talking about a vision from God. But it will apply to any vision. The scripture tells us to write the vision, goal, or plan down clearly so that others can understand what the vision is so they can accomplish the vision. Reviewing the building plans makes sure our vision is clear to the builder and us. That way, the builder will build the house we desired.

When I was discussing the process of building a new house, I was talking about the vision of the house we wanted to build. Having a guiding vision applies to building a home, a business, or a ministry. Accomplishing a vision often doesn't happen overnight. It might take months or years. But if we are patient, the vision will come to fruition.

What would a house look like if the planning was only verbal? You would tell the builder how you want the house to look. The builder would tell the subcontractor, and the subcontractor would tell his crew. Without plans, how many changes do you think would take place before completing the house?

We can have plans for building a house and other plans for our life. God also has a plan for your life, which He states in Jeremiah 29:11.

> For I know the thoughts *and* plans that I
> have for you, says the Lord, thoughts *and* plans
> for welfare *and* peace and not for evil, to give you
> hope in your final outcome. (Jeremiah 29:11
> AMPC)

What I love about this verse is not only does it tell us that God has a plan for our lives. But it also tells us that God's plan for our life is for good, our welfare, and peace and not for evil. Just as we had to develop plans so that the builder could build us a house, God has a plan for our life that He desires to give to us. God can give you a plan in great detail all at once or step-by-step as you proceed. God gave the plans for building the ark and the tabernacle in detail before the building began. The plan to get the Israelites out of Egypt and lead them through the wilderness was given to Moses step-by-step.

When planning, we have already seen that we should seek God's plan for our lives because He only wants good for us, and we should write our plans down. Whether planning a ministry, business, vacation, or war, we should get sound advice and count the cost, as discussed in Proverbs 20:18 and Luke 14:28–30.

> Plans are established by counsel; By wise counsel wage war. (Proverbs 20:18)

and

> v. 28 For which of you, intending to build a tower, does not sit down first and count the cost, whether he has *enough* to finish *it*—
> v. 29 lest, after he has laid the foundation, and is not able to finish, all who see *it* begin to mock him,
> v. 30 saying, "This man began to build and was not able to finish." (Luke 14:28–30)

Proverbs 20:18 tells us that our good plans are best with some form of good counsel. But if you are planning something major, make sure that you are receiving wise counsel. Our first counsel should be the Lord, no matter what we plan. For successful plans, Proverbs 16:3 says we are to commit our plans to the Lord so that our plans will come from Him and succeed. Verses 28–30 in Luke chapter 14 says to count the cost when planning. In these verses, Jesus is telling those following Him to count the cost of following Him. You also should count the cost of following Jesus and the cost to complete that which He has called you.

As you can see, planning is essential, but there is something you need to know about following God's plans and directions for your life. God is responsible for making them come to pass. People often choose and develop their plans and start working to have them come to fruition. However, when things don't go as planned, they decide to pray, asking God what they should do. God is not responsible for making your plans come to pass. Your plans are your responsibility. His plans are His responsibility. However, God can turn any situation into good.

We plan many things other than building a house. We plan ministries, businesses, vacations, weddings, families, and wars. There are different tools to accomplish our planning, such as blueprints, recipes, to-do lists, checklists, and schedules.

One of my favorite lists is the grocery list. Not because I make one when I go grocery shopping. But because my wife is so good at making one when we are about to grocery shop. If we go to more than one store, she will make a list for each store. We may purchase more than what is on the list, but we are sure to get the needed items on the list. When I go to the grocery store alone, I will not have a list unless she gives me a list. It is unlikely I will get everything I should when I go shopping by myself. Thus, the grocery list assists in assuring that I purchase the required products.

You can see why planning is essential, whether going to the grocery store or building a home. You are planning whether you use a blueprint, a list, a schedule, or a routine. That is why pilots use a checklist to ensure that everything is in proper working order before they take off to thirty-thousand-plus feet above the ground or why your car has recommended scheduled maintenance to keep it from breaking down at inconvenient moments.

Your Words

As seen in Genesis, God's spoken words have creative power. God in Genesis chapter 1 spoke things that didn't exist into existence. We also are told in Romans 4:17 about the creative power of words.

> (As it is written, I have made thee a father
> of many nations,) before him whom he believed,
> *even* God, who quickeneth the dead, and calleth
> those things which be not as though they were.
> (Romans 4:17 KJV)

Here we are told that God speaks as if things that don't exist do exist. That is what God was doing in the creation of this world. God was calling things that were not as though they were. God did this when He called Abram, a man with no children, *Abraham*, which means "the father of a multitude."

Because we were created in the image and likeness of God, our words also have creative power. Thus, just as God was deliberate in the words He spoke to create this world, so we should be deliberate in the words we speak. Because the words that we speak are essential in creating our world. Psalm 34:13 informs us that we can be deliberate in what we say because we can choose the words we speak.

> Keep thy tongue from evil, and thy lips
> from speaking guile. (Psalm 34:13)

The verse tells us that we can keep from speaking evil and guile things, which means that we can speak the truth and not false or deceitful words. Choose, therefore, to speak good and truthful things. Ephesians 4:29 also lets us know that we have a choice in what we speak.

> Let no corrupt word proceed out of your
> mouth, but what is good for necessary edifica-

tion, that it may impart grace to the hearers.
(Ephesians 4:29)

The word *let* in verse 29 implies that you have the ability to choose. You have the choice to choose evil and corrupt words or words that edify and impart grace to whom you are speaking. Both Psalm 34:13 and Ephesians 4:29 strongly indicate that people can control their speech. Ephesians 4:29 also informs us that the words we speak should impart grace to those that hear them. So when evil and false words want to come out of your mouth, hold your tongue and don't speak them. There have been many times that I have had to hold my tongue. Anyone who has lived any length of time has held their tongue at one time or another. Proverbs 18:21 indicates that the words we speak cause death or life.

Death and life *are* in the power of the
tongue, And those who love it will eat its fruit.
(Proverbs 18:21)

This verse says that our words can cause death in your life or things of life. You may remember as a child saying, "Sticks and stone may break my bones, but words will never hurt me." The truth is that sticks and stones can hurt you, but words will destroy you. The words you speak affect your life and also affect the lives of others. Just as your words affect others, other people's words can affect you. As for this creative power of words, James 3:2–12 gives an excellent description of how the words we speak control our lives.

v. 2 For we all stumble in many things. If
anyone does not stumble in word, he *is* a perfect
man, able also to bridle the whole body. (James
3:2)

This verse tells us that we can be a perfect man by simply controlling the words we speak. That is an amazing concept. People generally want to control themselves by controlling their physical actions. But God says that we control ourselves by controlling what we say, as discussed in James 3:3–6.

> v. 3 Indeed, we put bits in horses' mouths that they may obey us, and we turn their whole body.
>
> v. 4 Look also at ships: although they are so large and are driven by fierce winds, they are turned by a very small rudder wherever the pilot desires.
>
> v. 5 Even so the tongue is a little member and boasts great things. See how great a forest a little fire kindles!
>
> v. 6 And the tongue *is* a fire, a world of iniquity. The tongue is so set among our members that it defiles the whole body, and sets on fire the course of nature; and it is set on fire by hell. (James 3:3–6)

These verses compare our tongue to the bit in a horse's mouth, a ship's rudder, and fire. The bit in a horse's mouth and a ship's rudder indicate the tongue's ability to control our lives. The harness that we put on horses has a bit that goes into the horse's mouth. The reins of the harness control the bit. Pulling the reins to the left, right, or straight back, the rider can control the horse, a much larger and stronger animal. The rudder of a ship is a fraction of its size, yet it can turn the ship in circles. For example, the decommissioned aircraft carrier the USS *Enterprise* is 1,123 feet long, 252 feet wide, and weighs 94,780 tons. My thought, and perhaps yours, is what size rudder would efficiently maneuver a ship that size? I discovered that the *Enterprise* has four rudders, each weighing 35 tons, for a combined weight of 140 tons. These rudders are approximately 0.15% of the weight of the ship. Yet they efficiently turn the ship at the captain's demand. Just as our tongue turns our life through the words it speaks. The reference to the tongue being like fire speaks of the power of words to be destructive or productive. A spark can start a forest on fire and burn thousands of acres or can heat your home in the winter. A word spoken in anger can destroy your life and the life of those around you. A word of encouragement can motivate a person or a team to victory.

Verses 7 and 8 of James chapter 3 talk about man's ability to tame the tongue.

> v. 7 For every kind of beast and bird, of rep-
> tile and creature of the sea, is tamed and has been
> tamed by mankind.
> v. 8 But no man can tame the tongue. *It
> is* an unruly evil, full of deadly poison. (James
> 3:7–8)

Verse 7 tells us that man has tamed every creature on land, in the air, and in the sea. But verse 8 says that man has not been able to tame his tongue. I know that man has tamed, through training, the entire body. But we are told that man can't tame the tongue. Previously we have read scriptures that said the tongue could be controlled. There isn't a conflict between these scriptures. A man without the Holy Spirit and the renewing of his mind can't tame the tongue. But a man with the Holy Spirit and a renewed mind can tame the tongue. Verse 8 talks about the natural man, which cannot control the tongue. It is our born-again spirit that can control our tongue. Galatians 5:22–23 informs us of what our born-again spirit produces.

> v. 22 But the fruit of the Spirit is love,
> joy, peace, longsuffering, kindness, goodness,
> faithfulness,
> v. 23 gentleness, self-control. Against such
> there is no law. (Galatians 5:22–23)

Note that verse 23 says that one of the fruits of our born-again spirit is self-control. The Holy Spirit gives us the ability to control ourselves. This means that we can control the words that we speak. Like the bit in James 3:3, our spirit can control the direction of our life by controlling the words we speak. This control only comes from what we have received from Christ and who we are in Christ.

The following four verses of James chapter 3 discuss the inconsistency of man's tongue.

> v. 9 With it we bless our God and Father, and with it we curse men, who have been made in the similitude of God.
>
> v. 10 Out of the same mouth proceed blessing and cursing. My brethren, these things ought not to be so.
>
> v. 11 Does a spring send forth fresh *water* and bitter from the same opening?
>
> v. 12 Can a fig tree, my brethren, bear olives, or a grapevine bear figs? Thus no spring yields both salt water and fresh. (James 3:9–12)

These verses show that the words men choose to say vary between godly words and evil words. The words we speak should be consistently godly words. We shouldn't be injecting evil words into our speech. We shouldn't bless someone today only to curse them tomorrow.

A great New Testament example of the power of the words we speak is in Mark 11:12–14 and Mark 11:20–23.

> v. 12 Now the next day, when they had come out from Bethany, He was hungry.
>
> v. 13 And seeing from afar a fig tree having leaves, He went to see if perhaps He would find something on it. When He came to it, He found nothing but leaves, for it was not the season for figs.
>
> v. 14 In response Jesus said to it, "Let no one eat fruit from you ever again." And His disciples heard *it.* (Mark 11:12–14)

and

> v. 20 Now in the morning, as they passed by, they saw the fig tree dried up from the roots.
>
> v. 21 And Peter, remembering, said to Him, "Rabbi, look! The fig tree which You cursed has withered away."
>
> v. 22 So Jesus answered and said to them, "Have faith in God.
>
> v. 23 For assuredly, I say to you, whoever says to this mountain, 'Be removed and be cast into the sea,' and does not doubt in his heart, but believes that those things he says will be done, he will have whatever he says." (Mark 11:20–23)

This account of Jesus and the fig tree indeed shows the power of the words we choose to speak. In verses 12–14, Jesus finds a fig tree that has all the signs of a tree that should be bearing figs. Discovering that the tree had no figs, Jesus cursed the tree. In verses 20–23, while passing the tree in the morning, Peter noticed that the tree was dead. That is why in verse 23, Jesus tells His disciples that if a person were to tell a mountain to be cast in the sea, without a doubt in his heart, the mountain shall be cast into the sea. Jesus tells us that what we say with no doubt in our hearts will come to pass. If what we say without doubting will happen, we should be intentional and choose to speak only what we want to happen.

CHAPTER 7

Oops, You Made a Bad Choice

Are you born-again? If you are not, you have already made a bad choice, and you need to accept Jesus as your Lord and Savior. If you are born-again, you have chosen that which gives you everlasting life. You have made the choice that makes you a child of God and a joint-heir with Jesus Christ. Romans 10:9–10 tells you how to correct that bad choice of not being born-again.

> v. 9 That if you confess with your mouth
> the Lord Jesus and believe in your heart that God
> has raised Him from the dead, you will be saved.
> v. 10 For with the heart one believes unto
> righteousness, and with the mouth confession is
> made unto salvation. (Romans 10:9–10)

Two other New Testament verses, Acts 2:21 and Romans 10:13, say, "Whoever calls on the name of the Lord shall be saved." This calling on the name of the Lord, in effect, is the same as Romans 10:9–10. This calling is recognizing the Lordship and deity of Jesus. Verses 9 and 10 in Romans 10 tell us that salvation combines two simultaneous acts. You have to confess words indicating that Jesus is your Lord. While at the same time believing in your heart that Jesus rose from the dead.

confession + (while) believing = salvation

I like to emphasize the *while* because many people believe that they have salvation and are children of God because they believe in the one true God. Here is the thing about only believing in God.

> You believe that there is one God. You do
> well. Even the demons believe—and tremble!
> (James 2:19)

James informs us that demons and the devil, the chief demon, believe in God. Therefore, just believing in God puts you in some devilish company. Salvation comes from believing in Jesus and what He did for all mankind. Most unbelievers don't get rattled about the word *god*, but they dislike the name of Jesus. Even other religions have a god. Other religions believe that you must save yourself and don't have a savior. In John 14:6, Jesus informs us why we must believe in Him for salvation.

> Jesus said to him, "I am the way, the truth,
> and the life. No one comes to the Father except
> through Me." (John 14:6)

As you can see, if you don't accept Jesus, you will not have access to God. You have to speak your acceptance of Jesus, and you must believe what you are saying to receive salvation.

Salvation requires two correct steps at the same time to get saved. It is as simple as 1+1=2. We all know that 0+1=2 is incorrect, 0+1=1. Some people think that 0.01+1+1=2. These people like to add things to their belief in God, such as doing good deeds, giving money to the needy, going to church, etc. Many people believe they are saved because they belong to a specific denomination or go to church or confess the Lordship of Jesus but don't believe in the resurrection of Jesus. Remember that Romans 10:9 says you must believe in your heart that God has raised Jesus from the dead. Therefore, if one day in church or anywhere else you confess the Lordship of Jesus and don't believe that He rose from the dead, your words are empty, and you still have not obtained salvation. The importance of believing what you say is illustrated in Mark 11:23.

> For assuredly, I say to you, whoever says to this mountain, "Be removed and be cast into the sea," and does not doubt in his heart, but believes that those things he says will be done, he will have whatever he says. (Mark 11:23)

Before this verse, the disciples and Jesus passed by the fig tree that Jesus had cursed the day before. This verse states that the disciples now noticed that the tree had died. Jesus told the disciples to have faith in God. Jesus tells us that if we say for something to happen without doubting in our heart but believe that what we say will happen, it will happen. You have to choose to do two things at the same time. Speak and believe. Romans 10:10 says you must choose to believe in your heart while at the same time choosing to confess what you believe with your mouth. When you do these two things together, you will be born-again. If you are not born-again, here is a prayer to become born-again if you say it and believe it.

> God, I come and humble myself before You. I thank You for Jesus, who died for my sins and was resurrected from death so that I might have eternal life with You in heaven. I make Jesus the Lord and Savior of my life, now and forever. Amen.

Now, if you believe what you said, you are born-again. There will be times that you say oops after you say or do something, and you realize afterward that it was not of God. You might be thinking that now that you're born-again, you're not going to do anything wrong.

Since being born-again, I wish I could say that I have done everything correctly, but I can't. I don't know anyone who has. Romans chapter 3 says we all have sinned. That means that no person who has lived or will live on this earth other than Jesus has not sinned. Whenever we sin, it is a bad choice. So what are we to do when we do an oops (an ungodly choice)? We are to repent and follow God's way once again. Proverbs 24:16 tells us:

> For a righteous *man* may fall seven times
> And rise again, But the wicked shall fall by calamity. (Proverbs 24:16)

Even though I fall, or should I say choose contrary to God's way, I will repent, get up, and move forward. No matter how many times and how many ways I fall, I will get up, dust myself off, and start again. I like how Paul approaches this topic in Philippians chapter 3.

> v. 12 Not that I have already attained, or am already perfected; but I press on, that I may lay hold of that for which Christ Jesus has also laid hold of me.
> v. 13 Brethren, I do not count myself to have apprehended; but one thing *I do,* forgetting those things which are behind and reaching forward to those things which are ahead,
> v. 14 I press toward the goal for the prize of the upward call of God in Christ Jesus. (Philippians 3:12–14)

First, Paul notes that he is not perfect, yet he pursues the perfection Christ Jesus had attained for him. We also should be pursuing that which Christ Jesus had attained for us. What should you do about your oops moments? You should choose to forget your mistake, move forward, and pursue God's goal for you. From these verses by Paul and Proverbs 24:16, we know that when we choose a wrong action, we are to remind ourselves that we are not perfect and need to start over. When we choose to restart, we need to forget the wrong choice and press forward to the goal that Christ has set before us. We will also have to cast off any condemnation from the devil. Here is what Romans 8:1 says about that condemnation.

> *There is* therefore now no condemnation to
> those who are in Christ Jesus, who do not walk
> according to the flesh, but according to the Spirit.
> (Romans 8:1)

If you are in Christ Jesus and are walking according to the Word of God and step off your godly path and step for a moment on the path of your flesh, there is no condemnation from God. So don't let the devil condemn you when you are again on the path of righteousness. The devil brings condemnation by placing thoughts in your mind. These thoughts are designed to alienate you from God. The thoughts often start with how you have sinned and thus you can't possibly be a Christian. Followed by you are no longer in good standing with God, God can't help you now, and God will make you pay for that.

Proverbs 24:16 and Philippians 3:12–14 also inform us that we are to repent. Repenting is choosing to change one's mind. Here we will be talking about changing a person's evil thoughts and actions into godly thoughts and actions. Often when people talk about repenting, they talk about doing a 180-degree turn. I have made several 180-degree turns at the same spot several times. For example, when we first moved to Florida, when going home from a particular town square, I would get to Buena Vista Boulevard and make a right turn. I would drive about a half mile and see a golf course to my right and know I had turned in the wrong direction. With that knowledge, I chose to make a 180-degree turn. I usually am pretty good with directions, yet I made this mistake several times. Each time I went in the wrong direction, I chose to turn around and go in the other direction. I didn't decide that I would keep going in this direction since I was going this way. Nor did I condemn myself for going the wrong way. I told myself that I needed to pay closer attention so that

I make the correct turn. That is what we are to do when we have an oops moment. We are to get back on our correct path.

Earlier in the book, I discussed David's sin with Bathsheba in 2 Samuel 11. Now I will discuss King David's repentance for his sin of adultery and murder. I will compare David's repentance to King Saul's repentance for his rebellion and stubbornness in 1 Samuel 15. In 1 Samuel 15:3, God told Saul to go to war against Amalek.

> Now go and attack Amalek, and utterly destroy all that they have, and do not spare them. But kill both man and woman, infant and nursing child, ox and sheep, camel and donkey. (1 Samuel 15:3)

So Saul went to war against the Amalekites. Verses 8 and 9 tell us what Saul and the people did when they went to war.

> v. 8 He also took Agag king of the Amalekites alive, and utterly destroyed all the people with the edge of the sword.
> v. 9 But Saul and the people spared Agag and the best of the sheep, the oxen, the fatlings, the lambs, and all *that was* good, and were unwilling to utterly destroy them. But everything despised and worthless, that they utterly destroyed. (1 Samuel 15:8–9)

God told Saul, in verse 3, to utterly destroy Amalek. To "kill both man and woman, infant and nursing child, ox and sheep, camel and donkey." Verses 8 and 9 tell us that the children of Israel killed all the Amalekites except Agag, the king, and they spared the best of their animals. Samuel confronts Saul about his disobedience to the commands of God. We will jump ahead to verses 20–26.

> v. 20 And Saul said to Samuel, "But I have obeyed the voice of the LORD, and gone on

the mission on which the Lord sent me, and brought back Agag king of Amalek; I have utterly destroyed the Amalekites.

v. 21 But the people took of the plunder, sheep and oxen, the best of the things which should have been utterly destroyed, to sacrifice to the Lord your God in Gilgal."

v. 22 So Samuel said: "Has the Lord *as great* delight in burnt offerings and sacrifices, As in obeying the voice of the Lord? Behold, to obey is better than sacrifice, *And* to heed than the fat of rams.

v. 23 For rebellion *is as* the sin of witchcraft, And stubbornness *is as* iniquity and idolatry. Because you have rejected the word of the Lord, He also has rejected you from *being* king."

v. 24 Then Saul said to Samuel, "I have sinned, for I have transgressed the commandment of the Lord and your words, because I feared the people and obeyed their voice.

v. 25 Now therefore, please pardon my sin, and return with me, that I may worship the Lord."

v. 26 But Samuel said to Saul, "I will not return with you, for you have rejected the word of the Lord, and the Lord has rejected you from being king over Israel." (1 Samuel 15:20–26)

Verses 8 and 21 again give a clear picture of Samuel and the people's sin. In verse 22, Samuel tells Saul that God would rather have them obey His commands than sacrifice animals in disobedience. Our first choice should always be to obey God rather than sacrifice something after being disobedient. Verse 25 is Saul's feeble attempt to repent. When you don't have a repentant heart, any attempt at repentance will be weak and will not be accepted. Saul admits that he disobeyed God, but in doing so, he does not accept responsibility but blames his fear of the people. Saul chose to do that which we should never do. Saul chose to fear people over honoring God. The consequence of Saul's lack of repentance in verse 26 was the loss of being king over Israel.

Now we will discuss David's sin and repentance in 2 Samuel chapters 11 and 12. In chapter 11 of 2 Samuel, David is confronted by Nathan about his adultery with Bathsheba, the wife of Uriah (one of David's most loyal commanders). What happened was Bathsheba became pregnant, and David called Uriah home from the battle, believing that when Uriah arrived home, he would sleep with his wife, allowing David to cover up the affair. However, Uriah is more honorable than David and would not go home to his wife because Uriah believed it would be wrong to enjoy the comfort of his wife when his men were on the battlefield. Because Uriah wouldn't sleep with his wife, David still needed to cover up his sin. So to cover up his sin, David sent a sealed command to the commander of the battle to send Uriah into the hottest area of fighting and then withdraw the men from Uriah. Uriah's dying in the battle allowed David the opportunity to cover up his sin with Bathsheba. In chapter 12, the prophet Nathan tells David a story about a poor man whom a rich man greatly wronged. We will start reading here in verse 5.

> v. 5 So David's anger was greatly aroused against the man, and he said to Nathan, "*As* the LORD lives, the man who has done this shall surely die!
>
> v. 6 And he shall restore fourfold for the lamb, because he did this thing and because he had no pity."
>
> v. 7 Then Nathan said to David, "You *are* the man! Thus says the LORD God of Israel: 'I anointed you king over Israel, and I delivered you from the hand of Saul.
>
> v. 8 I gave you your master's house and your master's wives into your keeping, and gave you the house of Israel and Judah. And if *that had*

been too little, I also would have given you much more!

v. 9 Why have you despised the commandment of the LORD, to do evil in His sight? You have killed Uriah the Hittite with the sword; you have taken his wife *to be* your wife, and have killed him with the sword of the people of Ammon.

v. 10 Now therefore, the sword shall never depart from your house, because you have despised Me, and have taken the wife of Uriah the Hittite to be your wife.'

v. 11 Thus says the LORD: 'Behold, I will raise up adversity against you from your own house; and I will take your wives before your eyes and give *them* to your neighbor, and he shall lie with your wives in the sight of this sun.

v. 12 For you did *it* secretly, but I will do this thing before all Israel, before the sun.'"

v. 13 So David said to Nathan, "I have sinned against the LORD." And Nathan said to David, "The LORD also has put away your sin; you shall not die." (2 Samuel 12:5–13)

David was outraged toward the rich man in verses 5 and 6. And in verse 7, Nathan informed David that he was the man that had done evil in the sight of the Lord. In verses 10 through 12, Nathan informs David of the consequences of his sin. David thought that what he had done was in secret. But God knows our actions and our innermost thoughts. David repents in verse 13, telling Nathan, "I have sinned against the LORD." David made no excuses. He simply confessed his sin and that the sin was against the Lord. Nathan then informed David that the Lord had put away his sin and wouldn't be taking his life.

Both King Saul and King David were confronted by the prophet of their day about their sin. Yet we find two different responses. Saul made excuses and blamed the people for his sin. This sounds quite similar to what Adam said about Eve. Or maybe how you sound after you have made an oops. However, David took full responsibility for his sin and noted that it was a sin against God. That is what Joseph said about why he wouldn't lay with his master's wife. Joseph said that it would be a sin against his master and a sin against God. Both David and Joseph remind us that our sins are sins against God.

What is your response when you sin? Do you consider it a sin against another person, or do you consider it a sin against God? Do you make excuses, or do you confess and take responsibility for the sinful choice? If you make excuses or blame others, you have chosen not to repent.

I want you to know that there are a couple of oops from which you can't repent. Those oops are blasphemy against the Holy Spirit and taking the mark of the beast. We read in Matthew chapter 12 what the Bible says about blasphemy against the Holy Spirit.

> v. 31 Therefore I say to you, every sin and blasphemy will be forgiven men, but the blasphemy *against* the Spirit will not be forgiven men.
>
> v. 32 Anyone who speaks a word against the Son of Man, it will be forgiven him; but whoever speaks against the Holy Spirit, it will not be forgiven him, either in this age or in the *age* to come. (Matthew 12:31–32)

Verse 31 distinguishes between two types of sin that have to be forgiven. The two types of sins are acts contrary to God's desire, just called sin here, and the speaking of evil words, here called blasphemy. Interestingly, it says that every sin and blasphemy that a person does can be forgiven except one. That unforgiven sin is blasphemy against the Holy Spirit. Verse 32 says that if you speak evil against Jesus, it will be forgiven. Please note that this forgiveness is based on you receiving Jesus as Lord and Savior. But the verse says that if you speak evil against the Holy Spirit, you will never, never, never be forgiven. Here your mouth can steer you straight to hell.

Blasphemy is slander, detraction, injurious speech to someone's good name, and reproachful speech injurious to divine majesty. So if you speak reproachfully, that is to criticize the Holy Spirit, it will not be forgiven. Mark 3:28–30 makes this even more evident.

> v. 28 "Assuredly, I say to you, all sins will be forgiven the sons of men, and whatever blasphemies they may utter;
> v. 29 but he who blasphemes against the Holy Spirit never has forgiveness, but is subject to eternal condemnation"—
> v. 30 because they said, "He has an unclean spirit." (Mark 3:28–30)

Verse 30 tells us the reproachful speech was scribes saying in Mark 3:22 that Beelzebub (the devil) had possessed Jesus and that through the devil, Jesus was casting out demons. The only mercy for this oops is found in 1 Timothy 1:12–13.

> v. 12 And I thank Christ Jesus our Lord who has enabled me, because He counted me faithful, putting *me* into the ministry,
> v. 13 although I was formerly a blasphemer, a persecutor, and an insolent man; but I obtained mercy because I did *it* ignorantly in unbelief.

Paul indicates in these verses that he had been a blasphemer, but he was shown mercy because he did it ignorantly in unbelief. Meaning that you are eternally condemned if you are an ignorant believer and blaspheme the Holy Spirit. Those believers who aren't ignorant and could speak reproachfully of the Holy Spirit are mature believers.

We all know that what we say can get us into trouble, but in this case, what you say can put you in eternal damnation. There is also an action that can place you into eternal damnation. That action is taking the mark of the beast (the mark, name, or number of the beast, which is discussed in the book of Revelation). The following sections of scripture will give you some understanding of the mark of the beast and what becomes of those who take the mark.

> v. 16 He causes all, both small and great, rich and poor, free and slave, to receive a mark on their right hand or on their foreheads,
> v. 17 and that no one may buy or sell except one who has the mark or the name of the beast, or the number of his name. (Revelations 13:16–17)

We are told in these passages that it will not matter how great you think you are, how much money you have, or your living status. You will be required to receive the mark of the beast. It will not matter if you live in a country where you are considered free or in a country where you are considered property of the state; you will be required to receive the mark of the beast or face the consequences. Those consequences will be severe. Not being able to buy food, water, electricity, or gas means that you will not be able to purchase the things you need to survive in this world. Not having the ability to sell tells us that you will not have the capability to earn money to buy what you need for survival. Even if you live off the grid, eventually, you will need something. Then there is Revelation 14:9–11, which describes what will happen if you take the mark of the beast.

> v. 9 Then a third angel followed them, saying with a loud voice, "If anyone worships the beast and his image, and receives *his* mark on his forehead or on his hand,
> v. 10 he himself shall also drink of the wine of the wrath of God, which is poured out full strength into the cup of His indignation. He shall be tormented with fire and brimstone in the presence of the holy angels and in the presence of the Lamb.

> v. 11 And the smoke of their torment ascends forever and ever; and they have no rest day or night, who worship the beast and his image, and whoever receives the mark of his name." (Revelation 14:9–11)

As you read Revelation 14:9–11, you will see that the outcome of receiving the mark is eternal torment. God's wrath of fire and brimstone will be poured out on all receiving the mark on their forehead and hand. The verses say that "who worship the beast and his image, and whoever receives the mark of his name" will be tortured. It tells me that everyone that desires to avoid God's torment must choose to take a stand. There will not be any incognito believers. Incognito believers are those people that say they are believers but accept the ways of the world to get along with everyone. Believers will have to choose to have the conviction of Shadrach, Meshach, Abednego, and Daniel. Shadrach, Meshach, and Abednego refused to fall to their knees and worship the golden image that King Nebuchadnezzar had made. They knew that they would be thrown into a fiery furnace for not worshiping the golden image. Yet they chose only to worship the God who they served. Daniel chose to continue his daily prayer habits to God and not worship King Darius while knowing of the death sentence of being thrown into a den of lions. Shadrach, Meshach, Abednego, and Daniel rejected the worship of things or man and received death rather than rejecting their God. Keep in mind that Shadrach, Meshach, and Abednego didn't know that Jesus would show up in the fire and save them, nor did Daniel know that God would shut up the mouths of the lions. They were genuinely ready to die for their God. If you live in this world where receiving the mark is required to buy or sell, you will have to choose death to avoid God's wrath. You will find in Revelation 20:4–5 what will happen to those who refuse to receive the mark of the beast.

> v. 4 And I saw thrones, and they sat on them, and judgment was committed to them. Then *I saw* the souls of those who had been beheaded for

their witness to Jesus and for the word of God,
who had not worshiped the beast or his image,
and had not received *his* mark on their foreheads
or on their hands. And they lived and reigned
with Christ for a thousand years.

     v. 5 But the rest of the dead did not live
again until the thousand years were finished.
This *is* the first resurrection. (Revelation 20:4–5)

Shadrach, Meshach, Abednego, and Daniel were saved while in their death sentence. But these two verses make it clear that those who refuse to receive the mark of the beast will die in their death sentence of beheading. The scriptures tell us the souls of those who died for their stand against the beast and their belief in Jesus will for a thousand years reign with Christ, and those that receive the mark will remain dead for that thousand years.

I have talked about repentance, blasphemy of the Holy Spirit, and the mark of the beast. Now I want to discuss an oops that is easy to fall into. That oops is forgetting why you are here in this world. To start this section, I will tell you about a dream I had that illustrates how believers forget why they are here in this world.

The dream was about two girls that wandered off during a softball tournament. When it was nearing time for their game to start, someone told the coach that his catcher was not going to be able to make it to the game and asked the coach where the other players were. The coach had to go off and search the fairgrounds to find the two players before the game started, or the team would have to forfeit the game. Both players were players the team picked up just for the tournament, and both were second-base players. The team's catcher wasn't coming to the game, so one of these players would have to play catcher. When the coach found them, they were having a great time at another section of the fairgrounds. The purpose for which they were at the fairgrounds was not on the girls' mind. They chose to volunteer to play for the team and should have made that their priority. But they decided that they wanted to enjoy the other activities at the fairgrounds.

As a born-again believer, you have volunteered to become a member of God's family. Unlike Jesus, who said, "I must be about My Father's business," we often find ourselves about our own business. Like the two softball players, we can get distracted by the pleasures of this world and forget our purpose for being in this world.

As a born-again believer, you might think that the best thing that could happen to you would be to get born-again and immediately go to heaven. That might be the best thing for you but not for other people. When you are born-again, you and Jesus are spiritually one, and you were adopted into God's family. Also, you become a representative or ambassador of the family. As an ambassador, you are representing God. And as a representative of God, your priority should be the things of God. We are to be about our Father's business. You have the opportunity to determine what type of representative you will be. You can be an obedient ambassador or a self-absorbed ambassador focused on the pleasures of this world. If the two players in the dream were like many Christians today, every time it would be their time at bat, the coach would have to search for them. Does God have to search for you when He has an assignment for you?

You must remember that you are now members of God's family and that Jesus is our example. If you have been an older brother or sister, you most likely were told that you were to be an example to your younger brother or sister. For us, Jesus is like that older brother because He is our example of how to live our lives as believers. In Matthew 16:24, Jesus told us what we must do to follow His example.

> Then Jesus said to His disciples, "If anyone desires to come after Me, let him deny himself, and take up his cross, and follow Me." (Matthew 16:24)

If you desire to follow Jesus, you must choose to deny your wants, desires, and personality and choose to take up your cross. Your cross is your commitment to God's will for your life. Taking your cross will mean enduring persecutions, suffering, and perhaps even death. That is the only way you will be able to be like Jesus and perform God's will for your life.

In the fifth chapter of John, Jesus told us how he and, therefore, we are to represent the Father.

> v. 19 Then Jesus answered and said to them, "Most assuredly, I say to you, the Son can do nothing of Himself, but what He sees the Father do; for whatever He does, the Son also does in like manner.
>
> v. 20 For the Father loves the Son, and shows Him all things that He Himself does; and He will show Him greater works than these, that you may marvel. (John 5:19–20)

Jesus tells us that he does only the things that the Father is doing and, in the same way as the Father does, also that the Father shows the Son, whom He loves, everything that the Father is doing. Jesus performed all that the Father showed Him to do. In like manner, we are to do the same thing. In John 13:13–15, Jesus told us that He is our example. Jesus had washed the feet of the disciples after the Passover supper just before verse 13.

> v. 13 Ye call me Master and Lord: and ye say well; for *so* I am.
>
> v. 14 If I then, *your* Lord and Master, have washed your feet; ye also ought to wash one another's feet.
>
> v. 15 For I have given you an example, that ye should do as I have done to you. (John 13:13–15)

Jesus told the disciples that He was their example, and they were to do the things that He had done to each other. In like manner, we also should do the things the Bible tells us we are to be doing. In the eleventh chapter of 1 Corinthians, Paul encourages believers to follow him.

> Be ye followers of me, even as I also *am* of
> Christ. (1 Corinthians 11:1 KJV)

Paul lets us know that he is a disciplined follower of Christ, and we should follow or imitate him. Paul's condition for our following him is that we should follow him only as he follows Christ. Paul tells us that we can have as examples other people as long as their example is Jesus and that Jesus is our ultimate example. To follow the example Jesus has set for us is a choice. That choice matters more than any other choice. But every choice we make matters. I have talked about several choices people in the Bible made. God inspired men to write these and many other choices to give us examples of what to do and not to do. Let the Word of God and the Holy Spirit guide you to make God-honoring choices in your life.

ACKNOWLEDGMENTS

I am thankful for the support of my wife, Annette. Her input assisted me in clarifying some sections of *You Choose*. I also thank Annette for writing about the choice she made when Candace swallowed the earring. I thank Rick McFarland, pastor of River Rock Church and instructor at Charis Bible College, for his encouragement after reading a rough draft of the book. I am also thankful for suggestions of some great friends.

ABOUT THE AUTHOR

James was born-again at the age of thirty-two at Bethel Pentecostal in Grand Rapids, Michigan, and had a successful medical and surgical sales career. After retirement, James and his wife, Annette, attended Charis Bible College to gain greater insight into God's Word and develop a closer relationship with Him. Having obtained his goal, James desires that believers know what God has given His people and that the best way is always God's way.